Billene Seyoum Woldeyes

Transformative Spaces

MASTERS OF PEACE

edited by the

UNESCO Chair for Peace Studies
of the University of Innsbruck / Austria

Volume 10

LIT

Billene Seyoum Woldeyes

Transformative Spaces

Enabling Authentic Female Leadership through Self Transformation

The Case of AWiB

LIT

Bibliographic information published by the Deutsche Nationalbibliothek
The Deutsche Nationalbibliothek lists this publication in the Deutsche Nationalbibliografie; detailed bibliographic data are available in the Internet at http://dnb.d-nb.de.

ISBN 978-3-643-90502-4

A catalogue record for this book is available from the British Library

Klosbachstr. 107
CH-8032 Zürich
Tel. +41 (0) 44-251 75 05
Fax +41 (0) 44-251 75 06
E-Mail: zuerich@lit-verlag.ch
http://www.lit-verlag.ch

LIT VERLAG Dr. W. Hopf
Berlin 2014
Fresnostr. 2
D-48159 Münster
Tel. +49 (0) 2 51-62 03 20
Fax +49 (0) 2 51-23 19 72
E-Mail: lit@lit-verlag.de
http://www.lit-verlag.de

Distribution:

In the UK: Global Book Marketing, e-mail: mo@centralbooks.com
In North America: International Specialized Book Services, e-mail: orders@isbs.com
In Germany: LIT Verlag Fresnostr. 2, D-48159 Münster
Tel. +49 (0) 2 51-620 32 22, Fax +49 (0) 2 51-922 60 99, E-mail: vertrieb@lit-verlag.de

In Austria: Medienlogistik Pichler-ÖBZ, e-mail: mlo@medien-logistik.at
e-books are available at www.litwebshop.de

This book is dedicated to my beloved maternal grandmother, Elfenesh Mulatu, who left life on earth nineteen years ago. It is through her unexpected departure that I experienced my first deep trigger event for self-transformation at the young age of fourteen. Death from earthly life has been unable to break the strength of the bond we have as the values she espoused and the grace with which she existed is a vision close to my eyes every single day. Her protective and loving embrace, a sensation I experience every day from out beyond.

Shadow

You swept the dust and it sits in a ball behind the closet
The dust pan scrubbed clean hanging on a pedestal
And the tiny dirty crystals remain a residue in the sink
Testimony to the rinsing you've done
Because not all hearts carry clean crystals

You've painted over the old wounded patches
Not really scraping off the peeled paint
But the white and yellow you draw hide it well
After all who cannot smile at daisies?

The pretty rug you brought in - it lays dauntlessly
In the middle of your secret
Covering the splinter of your troubled history
With new stories of Persian old maidens
Gathered around sheep wool
knotting and weaving yarns of novelty

last summer you bought that huge African mask
its orange and brown wooded frame
now rests over the hollow of your spirit
by day your white friends tell you how ethnically beautiful it is
by night you sit across staring through its eyes
at the lonely hole it masks so well

and one rainy afternoon of your house warming
your cat dragged out the ugly dust ball from behind the closet
and cast it by your neighbours feet
and as your cousin leaned against the flowered wall
the paint cracked and revealed the hidden but raw patches
and while your friends pulled aside the Persian rug to set dance to your floor
the splinter of your wounded history rose up

later that evening you gathered them around the crackling fire
and with orange flames singing behind you
you pulled down the tribal mask
and what they saw was a human story
of a temporarily dishevelled spirit
and a yester year wound still fresh and raw

wrapped around the white bleached gauze
you bought this morning from the corner store
but didn't your grandmother tell you that
you can't clean old wounds with new gauze?

- Billene Seyoum Woldeyes (January 2014)

Acknowledgements

Many people have made the finalization of this work possible even through times when I had very little motivation left in me to tread ahead from its initial design and finalization as thesis work towards the work related in transforming it to a book. My mother, Aster Kebede, whose unrelenting words of encouragement have pushed me forward during hard times. My father, Seyoum Woldeyes, whose humour and playfulness provided the much needed balance to be struck between play and work. My advisor, Dr. Wolfgang Dietrich who patiently waited on me to explore and decide when the timing for me was right to deliver my work. His flexibility and presence throughout the two and half year of starting, stopping, changing a topic and finally writing and delivering has been heart-warming to say the least.

I want to also extend my gratitude to my brothers Teddy and Brook, my mentor in Canada Sabrina Ali, and my wonderful friends in Addis who suffered my many absences when I got engaged in the writing process. And finally all of the people I have encountered over the past three and half years since returning to Ethiopia, who have greatly contributed to an eye-opening experience through which I navigate my *self*-transformation and the prism through which I conducted my analysis.

~

TABLE OF CONTENTS

PREFACE

This book has come to fruition from its original version written as a thesis for a Master's degree in Peace and Conflict Studies. Having experienced a few deep-trigger events for self-transformation over the course of my life, the presence phase of study while in attendance at the University of Innsbruck, Austria enabled me to take stock of and clearly articulate what these personal experiences of transformation were. The presence phase experience itself was a deep-trigger event in its non-mainstream approach to peace studies and a bedrock for clarifying my long time interest in *self*-development as tool for positive change.

What you will find in the ensuing pages is my analysis of why and how transformative spaces are powerful in positively affecting women and their communities. This analysis is rooted in an honest account of how I transformed while co-creating and sustaining a transformative space for other women in my community.

In his book entitled The Seat of the Soul, Gary Zukav underlines that no one amongst us is an expert on the human experience and that it is our sharing of what we perceive that would hopefully help others on their journey. What is contained in this book is precisely a sharing of perception and a paradigm that has enabled positive transformation in other women and myself. It is my hope that those in whose hands it falls will find it useful in their *self*-transformation journey towards becoming an authentic leader.

Love & Light,

Billene Seyoum Woldeyes
March 30, 2014
Addis Ababa, Ethiopia

LIST OF ACRONYMS

AI	Appreciative Inquiry
AWiB	Association of Women in Business
EI	Emotional Intelligence
EPRDF	Ethiopian People's Revolutionary Democratic Front
EOTC	Ethiopian Orthodox Tewahedo Church
NVC	Non Violent Communication
UNOCHA	United Nations Office for Coordination of Humanitarian Affairs

GLOSSARY OF AMHARIC WORDS

Amharic: a language of the Amhara ethnic group of northern Ethiopia and the official working language of the country.

Ethiopiawinet: norms related to an Ethiopian identity.

Iddir: burial societies.

Iqub: traditional credit associations.

Mahiber: religiously based or neighbourhood based associations.

Toffa: clay cooking pot.

Wondata: word denoting mannerisms to be "like a man"; mostly uttered on occasions of success.

Yilugnta: word which is used to denote a state of waiving one's own immediate needs in favor of that of others so as to preserve harmony and save face.

CHAPTER ONE

The authentic self is the soul made visible ~ Sarah Ban Breathnach

1. My Perspective as An Author

I am an Ethiopian female by birth and a Canadian by citizenship. I am the last born of three children and the only daughter in our nuclear family, granting me advantages as well as burdensome responsibilities that I have continually negotiated throughout my life. I have spent almost half of my life outside of my birth country Ethiopia. Nevertheless, some norms of *Ethiopiawinet* (Ethiopianess) injected in me through socialization have sustained themselves throughout the years. Some characteristics of what I refer to as *Ethiopiawinet* is a concoction of tradition, superstition, pride, faith, patriotism, community, festivity, religion, ethnicity, passivity, rigid notions of right and wrong, reservation, aggression, endurance, suppression, masks and socially defined gender roles and identities.

I grew up in the push and pull of duality – my nature versus my nurture dipped in the bitter sweetness of *Ethiopiawinet*. Girlhood had its own pleasures and challenges as I traversed the plains of what it meant to be a "good Ethiopian girl". Being socialized into an Ethiopian girl then woman has for me been riddled with the fallacies of culture. I have often struggled to squirm my way out of suffocating norms of what to say, how to say it, what not to do, what to wear, how, when and whom to date, to befriend, keeping in line with what was "culturally acceptable".

While now I may come as a shock, a nuisance, or maybe an inspiration to my friends, family and those around and beyond me, I take great pleasure in creating, living and sharing an authentic life doing the things I love to do with those I choose to do them with. I consider myself lucky to be in a privileged position of making my own simple choices and acting upon them.

I have never been fond of labels and their claustrophobic capacity to box people and their identities into since I believe that identities are not static and are continuously shifting, changing and evolving as we interact with the multitude around us. However, there are three identity subsets that are important to me and that influence the focus of this book and as a result it becomes necessary to explain them and why they matter to me. Additionally, it will also be important to discuss the influences that have shaped me into the person I am today as well as the experiences that add value and purpose to my thematic interest.

1.1 IDENTITIES

1.1.1 *Self*-Identity

1.1.1.1 Ethiopian Girl to Woman

My identification as Ethiopian has less to do with patriotic and nationalistic tendencies. Rather, this has more to do with the norms and traditions that I grew up around which I can associate with a group of people that I share some of the same experiences with. I have continuously challenged some of these norms and traditions from an early age through my own processes of what felt authentic and inauthentic to me. So why assume these norms as components of what make up my identity if I have been challenging them? Well, in order to discuss experiences of exercising authentic female leadership in Ethiopia, I have to address those very elements that have been a component of my own struggles to transform out of what stifles and into what liberates as a girl evolving into a woman.

I recall the latter part of my girlhood was somewhat informed by the fallacies of culture I refer to earlier wherein the virtues of what made for a good girl were pre-defined. There were ways to be a girl and if those standards were not kept then the societal consequences would be shaming. Therefore, I grew up enclosed within the fear of not expressing my needs and opinions for fear of not being taken seriously and because "nice" girls did not disagree or disobey.

Subservience and obedience was the norm and she that went out of these boundaries was an embarrassment to her family. At age fifteen, I remember when a geography teacher at the school I attended came across my friend and me singing out loud and being theatrical inside our classroom during break time. Chastising us for the behaviour, he vowed to tell my parents of this "craziness" which put me in tears the whole day for fear that I had disappointed my parents and that my "un-girly" behaviour had brought shame to them. Bound by such examples and expectations of girl identity in Ethiopia, I felt from a young age resistance percolate within me.

1.1.1.2 Feminist

The spirit of resistance that permeated my girl identity was sourced in the traditional "can" and "cannot" divide sanctioned by most of society. As a young girl, Church convention had it that during my monthly cycle I was "impure" and therefore cannot enter the grounds. I would enter anyhow. Visits to households where elders who had received communion that day would entail refraining from physical contact with the elder or his/her belonging if menstruating. I would anyhow. For me this silent disobedience was symbolic of rejecting the notion of "impurity" and "dirtiness" associated with the singular element defining my femininity and transition to another stage of girlhood. Of course at that age I did not have the critical lens with which I approach it now, but even without the intellectual words to convey those thoughts growing up I still grappled with similar examples of gender asymmetry. Such examples of questioning the status quo would later in life lead me to a paradigm that gave me the words to better articulate what I was resisting at a young age. This paradigm was feminism.

One afternoon in 2010 a friend and classmate asked me which school of feminist thought I identified with. It did not take me long to provide an answer since in the preceding days I had been engrossed in this contemplation and decided that feminism for me was not a dogma, a code of conduct or rules by which I must abide by and that from each school of thought there were things I agreed and disagreed with. Simply put feminism, for me, is an acknowledgement that a system driven by antiquated cultural norms has been of great disservice to a grouping of people and that this system needs an overhaul to bring into balance the perspectives, needs, choices, abilities, voices and contributions of both groupings, male and female without preference, repression and domination of one over the other.

Although this identification with feminism has been an on-going process for me, it has become a much more important aspect of the person I am today and which informs the way I perceive everything around me. Firstly, unlike the widely held perspective that feminism is about male bashing, for me it is not about hating men as opposed to the prevailing and erroneous assumption. Secondly, I do not view feminism as an ideology engaged in breaking down family ties. When there is an underlying imbalance in any type of relationship, awareness by one party of that imbalance and taking steps to re-imagine the existing dynamic can and will introduce tremendous change that the other party may perceive as threatening. Therefore, feminism is about bringing the awareness to women that the choices and possibilities they have in their lives are not biologically pre-determined and empowering them in exploring ways that they can live to their full potential.

Lastly, my definition of feminism negates the notion that these ideas are Western. I do not find women's freedom to choose the life they will to live and equality of opportunity as un-African or un-Ethiopian, even though that is the argument that is raised when as an Ethiopian woman, I identify as a feminist. It is through this feminist lens that I evaluate culture, tradition, values, and norms in my analysis. Beyond my research interests and objectives, feminism is also a way of life that utilizes a particular lens to understand the effects on and differences of systems, processes, and institutions between women/girls and men/boys.

1.1.1.3 Activist

Activism is also an important aspect of the person that I am today. Personally, activism means the processes, activities I engage in and tools that I utilize to share and create awareness about gender issues that I perceive as having been marginalized and drowned in rhetoric. To be an activist is to use the tools within my capacity towards engaging in dialogue for social change with those that are within my sphere of influence. To this end the tools that I utilize at the moment are poetry, blogging and active engagement with women's associations.

1.1.2 Leader identity

It is not until very recently that I began to see my*self* as a leader. Previously, my concept of leadership was premised upon the notion that leaders were found primarily at the top of the career ladder, held domain over knowledge and made no mistakes. I believe such a concept evolved from the top-down educational and social culture I was socialized into. Although I have been in a place of positional leadership since the age of nineteen at the helm of my first professional job, the realization that I too was can be a leader with conscious cultivation of leadership skills dawned on me in conversation with my former supervisor. His belief in my leadership abilities and potential challenged me to overcome my own insecurities and the mental barrier I had erected in understanding that a leader was not without blunders. Rather, that the integrity with which he/she overcame the blunders was what made the leader.

Dismantling the concept of perfection that I had spun around what it meant to be a leader made me appreciate how everyone, including me, exercised leadership in the many facets of our lives. And therefore, my leadership identity is one that I find continuously unravelling itself through daily encounters experienced in the various roles I play. As a daughter, sister, friend, employee, colleague and the many other roles I assume, the most important guiding element has been that my actions and interactions are in alignment with my values.

1.1.3 Spiritual identity

As is the case for some people, my spiritual identity evolved through a period of my life in which I was experiencing intense transformation, as does a reptile shedding skin. This transformative phase in my life shook up the thoughts and ideas I had developed as the basic and unchanging tenets of my existence and the world around me. However, it became apparent that those tenets were never rooted in *self*-awareness because they eventually disintegrated in the face of challenge, forcing me to reinvent the person that I had carried with me. Part of this transformation included that of revisiting my spiritual identity.

I grew up under the influence of the Ethiopian Orthodox Tewahedo Church (EOTC). Ethiopia's culture and tradition is heavily influenced by religion and therefore, not only did the influence permeate my religious identity, but also that of my cultural identity and understanding of the world. Hierarchy, obedience, female subservience, repression, judgement and a highly defined conception of right and wrong is prevalent in the EOTC tradition, as is the case in other religious institutions. Growing up, although I enjoyed some of the religious traditions and found the other morals and beliefs entrenched in the Orthodox Church quite suffocating and archaic, the influence was strong in my formative years. The very polarized notion of right and wrong is what ultimately led me to the challenges I experienced which paved the way for my internal transformation.

I realized that a spiritual identity based on religious dogmas was not serving me anymore as in times of trials and tribulations, where I drew my strength and courage was from a source that defied dogmatic norms. The EOTC culture gives great weight to divine intervention in every facet of life. Divinity embodied in an all-knowing male God that passed judgment as he saw fit. Therefore, challenges in life were God's doing and the related solutions were to be delivered by "him". Later, during the first transformative encounter in my life, the friendship of a woman I consider my angel on earth cajoled me take ownership of my life and circumstances by identifying and realizing the sacred and divine within me and around me.

Therefore, today my spiritual identity is not grounded in a belief that God is of particular form or gender, deciding and determining outcomes for me. Rather, I operate from a place of taking ownership for my experiences, choices and the ability to transform the circumstances I find myself in towards a satisfactory result. Leaning more towards Eastern spiritual practices, my spiritual identity is an important component of the lens through which I understand what authentic leadership means.

1.2 Influences

There are a number of influences in my life that have shaped the journey into the person that I am today. These influences further explain how and why my topic of interest is personally relevant.

1.2.1 Family

I come from a middle-income family which has granted me privileges to experience my immediate surroundings and beyond in a manner that was different from the average person in Ethiopia during my formative years. My private school education, higher learning abroad and the opportunity to travel worldwide and come in contact with different paradigms afforded me the chance to peruse through different cultural and value systems while contrasting them alongside the dominant cultural story I grew up with, in the city of my birth Addis Ababa. Despite these stated privileges, I was still a girl slowly being woven into the strong fabric of pre-defined gender roles yet receiving mixed messages at home about what a girl should be like, which eventually would influence my understanding of leadership styles.

The messages were mixed because they did not fall within the strict confines of pre-determined roles as was exhibited at a social level. For example, my mother never forced upon me the idea of learning to cook because I was a girl. Meanwhile, girls my age were being socialized in their homes with the notion that to be a great Ethiopian homemaker, a girl/woman had to know how to take apart a whole chicken and make the traditional chicken stew to perfection. This knowledge set apart would be worthy "wives" from the ones that would not be able to "find" a husband. Because of this inherent association of knowing how to make chicken stew to being a "good wife" I resisted learning the recipe despite the fact that I loved to cook. And my mother never forced that knowledge upon me, accepting that my interest in food making was an artistic expression rather than a gender duty.

On the eve of holidays where women are traditionally in the kitchen preparing this stew, I would be at my father's side taking part in the slaughter and skinning of the festive sheep - a task that is culturally attributed to men.

Or other days, washing the car and changing the tires, to prove to my father that I could very well take the leadership and perform the tasks that were thought to be “manly”.

My parents did not raise me with the concept of becoming a “wife”. Rather I was groomed into independence spearheaded by pursuing education. It was of great importance to both my parents that I achieved the highest level of education and established a career before the consideration of marriage came into play. A strong personality in the family, I grew up watching my mother negotiate so many spaces with such tenacity and襲ferociousness that defied the strict gender norms prevalent in society. And therefore, for a long period in my life, she remained the exception rather than the rule.

1.2.2 Society

Norms of silences and multiple taboos around women and girls’ experiences define what it was like to grow up in an Ethiopian society of my generation and the ones before. There were and still are too many silences that surround the experiences of women and girls, in all spheres of our lives. A climate of overt double standards exists on how women and men perform gender. Men comprise most of the positions of leadership on all levels of the social structure while the role of subordination is indoctrinated into women and girls through various outlets. Although the agenda of the ruling party – the Ethiopian People’s Revolutionary Democratic Front (EPRDF) - over the past few years has been to push for gender equality through laying out various initiatives, these activities remain short of addressing the social roots of gender biases. Therefore, notions of female subservience prevail in most parts of the country thereby impacting the number of women seen in positional leadership.

Personally, I grew up adapted into the silence and taboos, not fully understanding all of them and rejecting some. Yet their existence and persistence through generations became a source of my curiosity to identify and tackle the source of these norms that not only stifled self-expression, but in my opinion were also the pillars of support that maintained the suppression of women and girls’ voices.

1.2.3 Women’s Organizing

Since my return to Ethiopia in late 2010, I became highly active in forms of women’s organizing that was within my reach. Through induction by one of Ethiopia's and world renowned gender justice advocates, I became engaged with a group of twelve women who were involved in setting up a bank aimed at increasing the number of women with economic ownership. Attributable to the discrimination experienced by women as it pertained to access to bank loans, the women I worked with were determined to address these issues by setting up a bank with female majority of shareholders, gender equal board representation and the design of institutional policies that were gender sensitive. During the twelve-month duration I worked with these women, I became aware of the many facets of Ethiopian women's lives as shared through the many stories expressed by the women organizing the bank. These consisted of stories of leadership, tenacity, violence, discrimination, and career hardships. I realized that the twelve women I was working closely with had defied the norm in their own spheres and were excelling in their lives. Through the privilege they had gained, they aimed to empower other underprivileged women economically by becoming the limited female voices in a male-dominated industry.

In their achievement of setting up the first all-female founded financial institution in the country which was gender equal in its leadership, I came to terms with how very little progress had been made in the country when it came to gender parity in positional leadership, and that enabling avenues for female leadership was crucial to fostering decision-making authority and capacity of Ethiopian women.

Around the same time that I began working with the women's bank group, I also started attending a monthly meet-up of women in business and in different professions. These monthly sessions revolved around creating a space for women to come together and discuss issues relevant to their professional and personal lives. The discussions that came up at the monthly meet-ups indicated that there were critical factors that nurture female leadership and how without them, the prospect of seeing many more women at the helm was farfetched. These critical factors pertained to cultural barriers that gave weight to female modesty, passivity and home-making over self and professional development - evidence of the predominance of a subservient attitude ingrained in Ethiopian women by way of culture.

My involvement with this association, Association of Women in Business (AWiB), transformed me from a semi-active participant to a very active board member at the helm of its presidency in 2013. Through engagement with AWiB, I witnessed my own transformation and that of others and the association itself, proving to me that one aspect of social change is strengthening female leadership by building personal and professional capacities. The approach that AWiB espouses is that of norm defiance – itself an approach that is quite dear to me as a product of a culture that I believe has conditioned both women and men to embody an existence of being inauthentic with each other, but primarily and most importantly, with ourselves.

In my two-year active encounter with AWiB, I have witnessed my interest in personal development and self-transformation grows each day. I have witnessed the power of a collective space become transformational. And it has become a space where I embraced an evolving *self* amidst the camaraderie of a group of women with the similar intention of transforming their environment by transforming themselves.

Although there are many facets to my being, what I have shared in this opening is a glimpse into the experiences and influences that have shaped my identity and which inform the thematic focus of this book.

~

CHAPTER TWO

Personal transformation can and does have global effects. As we go, so goes the world, for the world is us. The revolution that will save the world is ultimately a personal one. ~ Marianne Williamson

2. Introduction To The Topic

2.1 Purpose of the study

The purpose of this book is to explore authentic leadership and what is needed to cultivate it through *self*-transformation amongst urban Ethiopian women for effecting social change. With emphasis on cultivating positional leadership informed by authenticity, experiences of leadership in different roles will also be a focus of the ensuing pages.

2.2 Background

A wealth of the literature on leadership is predominantly contextualized within the business organizational setting. There is little coverage of the leadership exercised at a personal level and within an interpersonal context, devoid of an organizational affiliation. Furthermore, there is limited literature linking the practice of leadership with the larger goal of peace studies – that of attaining lasting peace beyond the dichotomous notions of negative and positive peace. Whereas the leadership capacities of those in power is analysed and discussed within the context of political and economic pitfalls experienced by a country or region, these discussions remain within the realm of complex hierarchical relationships that are object-centric rather than subject-centric. Additionally, the prevalent image of a leader falls within the male domain.

An historical and herstorical[1] overview of power distribution and its exercise in Ethiopia indicates that leadership was concentrated amongst the elite or ruling class, with the rest of the populace depicted as "masses who need

1 'Herstorical' refers here to women's accounts of their past where mainstream historical texts have not taken into account the missing information on women's voices, roles, participation.

guidance" and stripped of ownership and decision making over their personal domain. Of course, the dominant and documented narrative of leadership in the country's history is that of political and religious leadership; wherein the latter is hardly treated as separate and distinct from the former. Additionally, with the lack of documentation on women's role in the country's more than two thousand year history, available documents that attempt to broach the subject maintain a paradigm of female leadership exercised as wives and consorts – extensions of those in power rather than as individual actors (Bizuneh, 2001).

The current political regime, the Ethiopian People's Revolutionary Democratic Front (EPRDF) has espoused the notion of increasing the number of women in decision-making capacities since its ascent to political power in 1993 (Genene, 2003). This notion has been advanced by way of becoming signatory to various international and continental legal instruments that support the development of women's inclusion in key decision making arenas. Further to this agenda is the enhancement of women's leadership capacity by facilitating access to education and training. While these moves to enhance women's positional leadership capacity by emphasizing access to education is an important part of the equation, very little attention is being paid to another dimension of cultivating leadership capacities, which is person specific and *self*-transformation centric.

The dominant approach to enabling female leadership is heavily reliant on mainstream methods to education and hard skills acquisition, making the application of the technical know-how into the practical quite cumbersome. Therefore, it falls short of equipping women in the country with the *self*-reflective tools necessary to challenge some of the cultural and personal norms that infringe upon the will and power to exercise authentic leadership. Among the barriers of gender and leadership that Meron Genene identifies, cultural norms, the "glass" ceiling and a lack of female role models, are three points that will be further explored at depth in subsequent sections.

The problem with the current approach, as explained above, is that it is one-dimensional in that it looks only into the structural barriers to women's exercise of leadership. This is not to take away from the importance of correcting the structural disparities, which are also a key component of feminist approaches to development. Rather, the argument being made is that female leadership in Ethiopia can further be enhanced by incorporating a holistic perspective and approach, which includes transformation of the *self* through inquiry into culture, norms, identity, spirituality, personal stories and experiences. Otherwise, this single pronged approach risks maintaining the status quo, in its aim to cultivate female leadership, by extending a rudimentary way of exercising leadership.

2.3 Research Questions

In this top-down methodology of female leadership development guided by a political agenda that is heavily reliant on party affiliation or group-think (Biseswar, 2008), the opportunity for women to identify and nurture their personal authentic leadership capabilities is at risk. This is attributable to a socio-political environment that has limited the possibility of many civil society actors to create and sustain diverse platforms that enable deconstruction of social, political and economic norms. The absence of such far reaching platforms not only arrests the personal progress of the average woman in the country who is guided by a culturally sanctioned state approach to leadership development, but also retards the potential of nurturing change agents who directly and indirectly play a crucial role in fostering and maintaining peace.

Therefore, the questions that I aim to address in this work are threefold:

1. What are the components of authentic leadership and what type of *self*-transformation is required to be an authentic leader?
2. What is the dominant cultural narrative in Ethiopia that hampers authentic female leadership?
3. How can organized platforms enable *self*-transformation and authentic leadership among urban Ethiopian women?

I aim to answer these questions firstly by engaging in a discussion of the literature available on self-transformation and the newly emerging style of authentic leadership. Secondly, I will also discuss the research questions posed through sample responses given by women to a set of questions on authentic female leadership among urban Ethiopian women. And lastly, I will examine the work of a local association focused on female personal and professional development, using it as a case study.

2.4 Why Female Leadership?

The rational for focusing on female leadership in this work has emerged out of many conversations with other women that I have come in contact with. Through my involvement with AWiB and other encounters, I have learned that several aspects of culture are so ingrained in how women in urban settings negotiate the multitude around them. The norm is such that there is an underestimation of women's capacity for leadership – a perspective held by both sexes. Therefore, an act or deed performed by a woman and considered to be courageous is commended by declaring wondata – an Amharic word which means "like a man". Such a declaration in my opinion presupposes that leadership initiatives exemplified by women are perceived as scarce and therefore the cultural frame of reference is to polarize abilities and evaluate female accomplishments against culturally sanctioned male standards.

Therefore, in the choice of focusing on female leadership through self-transformation, I do not assume that authentic leadership in men is not deserving of attention. Rather, my aim is an attempt to deconstruct the dominant cultural narratives that impact women's authentic leadership abilities.

2.5 Significance of the study

This work takes on the point of view that the subject is not far removed from the object for which transformation is sought. By adopting a transpersonal and trans-rational lens through which this study is conducted the significance of the study is such that female leadership approaches in Ethiopia will not be viewed through a narrow lens of rationality only. Rather this study aims to contribute to the female leadership discussion in the country by offering a holistic and trans-rational perspective.

2.6 Definitions

The following terms will appear throughout this book and therefore I offer a brief introductory explanation to enable a closer and harmonized reading.

2.6.1 Trans-personal

The transpersonal refers to a transcendence of or a moving beyond and through the limitations experienced by the personal yet its starting point is the personal. Where the personal is situated in an identification with the egoic *self*, the transpersonal *self* rises above the masks of what make up an I amness moving towards a we-ness. Transcending the egoic *self* and the thinking mind entails letting go of false illusions and making a greater connection to deeper and higher aspects around and of the *self*. One gains a heightened awareness and consciousness of own intentions, thoughts, actions, beliefs, shadows, fears, needs, feelings and remains tuned in to subtle shifts in and around. In practicality, the authentic leader's work as a change agent begins by working on the *self*.

2.6.2 Trans-rational

Transrational refers to transcending rational thinking and experience forms yet still incorporating rationality as an element in a larger frame of reference. A transrational approach integrates the transpersonal, systemic ecological and spiritual perspectives.

2.6.3 *Self*

Within this book, *self* refers to the totality of body-soul-mind that make up a person as well as the higher being contained within, transcending limitations of personhood.

2.6.4 *Self* – Transformation

By *self*-transformation, I refer to the processes and experiences of becoming *self*-conscious and *self*-reflective. Moving away from functioning on auto pilot through life and towards purposeful and conscious living.

2.6.5 Authenticity

Authenticity refers to the quality of being truthful and honest in appearance and performance of the *self*. Bringing forth a congruence of espoused values and actual values.

2.7 Limitations

In its design, this work is limited to an exploration of the topic only within the context of an urban setting – more specifically in the capital city of Ethiopia - Addis Ababa. This is so, given that the case study association for the moment is targeting only those women who are in the capital city, have access to the Internet, who can communicate adequately in English and who are both entry and mid-level professional women. Therefore, the work is limited to the extent that a generalization of the findings to women in the whole country will be difficult.

Additionally, given the lack of written material and a wide intellectual discussion on authenticity and personal transformation, the literature and lens in use are derivatives of Western literature on the subject matter. However, the premise that this work makes is that at a basic human level cultural differentiations do not impact human consciousness and personal evolution.

The next chapter will scan the literature on authentic leadership and self-transformation.

~

CHAPTER THREE

Some will say, "I lead"; others, "We lead"; still others, "They did it through us." No matter which way we frame leadership, as we participate in it, we can all live and embody the truth into which authenticity invites us.

~ Bob Terry

3. State of the Art

3.1 Authenticity

The etymology of the word *Authentic* finds root in the Greek word *authentikos*. The English translation means “original, genuine, principal”. Composed of the two words *autos* and *hentes* which mean “*self*” and “worker, doer, being” respectively, the word *authentikos* is a by-product of the noun *authentes*. In studying the usage of the word (English-Word Information , 2012) in the English language, it is not until the late 18th century that it was employed to denote a state of being “genuine”.

In its many usages, the concept of *authenticity* is applied in various fields and sub-fields. Humanistic psychology (Maslow, Rogers), existential philosophy (Sartre, Heidegger), theories of spiritual leadership (Fry), social identity (Abrams & Hogg) and leader prototypicality (B. van Knippenberg), are some of the areas where the concept of *authenticity* is functional to elucidate human behaviour by their proponents. In the many applications to human behaviour however, a unifying element is the presence of *self* as the one that directs congruence, adherence and commitment to own declared values and beliefs.

Peter. F. Schmid states, “An authentic person, therefore, is his or her own ‘author’ in the relationship both to his or her*self*, and to others” (Schmid, 2012). In Schmid’s definition where authorship is inherent to being authentic, it is understood that an aspect of being an authentic person is that of taking ownership in how relationships and encounters are navigated. Many other thinkers including Peter F. Schmid have declared explanations of what authenticity is and who is authentic, as discussed here below:

“To live authentically means to live truthfully, i.e. in accordance with one’s deep convictions, beliefs, values and goals.” ~ Bo Jacobsen

In Jacobsen’s definition of authenticity, the central idea is that of truthfulness. Such a truth as derived not from established standards external to *self* (Jacobsen, 2007). Rather the *self* is prominent here again in this definition, whereby the individual is the driver and originator of which standards to be governed by and therefore acts and behaves in harmony with him*self*/her*self*.

"Inauthentic existence is moulded by external factors, whether they be circumstances, moral codes, political and religious authorities or other influences" ~ John Macquarrie

By the above definition of in-authenticity, John Macquarrie asserts that an authentic way of living is one that has examined its separation from being influenced by the external and making a clear and aware choice of living in alignment with that choice. The freedom inherent to authentic living is that the choice can be to follow the norm or to go against it, as long as it reflects the deepest values of the *self* (Jacobsen, 2007).

"Authenticity involves acknowledging and accepting all parts of the self, and acting in such a way that they function together as harmoniously as possible, with none repudiated or repressed." ~ Sean Sayers

In Sayers definition, intimate knowledge of *self* prevails, where such knowledge and personal understanding enables an alignment in articulation and manifestation of one's deepest values. His emphasis on none repudiation and repression of the *self*, supports Jacobsen's explanation and focus on truthfulness. Looking at truthfulness through Sayers definition, the truth embodied in authenticity is therefore derived as a result of full expression of *self*. In reviewing what can hinder such a full expression, Sayer further posits, "we can be true to ourselves only by emancipating ourselves from socially imposed roles" (Sayer, 2012) .

It is evident that authenticity requires recognizing the dilemma between following societal norms and remaining true to *self*. However, a cautionary note to be made in discussing authenticity against a normative social backdrop is introduced by Lehel Balogh. Balogh's argument is that the discrepancy could very well be that the process to "becoming authentic" itself could be culturally imposed as well. In a critical examination of the concept of authenticity and *self*, Balogh explains "the process of becoming ourselves is always a directed process. It is never me who first thinks about the need and necessity to "truly" become my*self*. The particular culture which I live in radiates the expectation through many channels that I shall become my*self*" (Balogh).

An existentialist approach to authenticity conveys that we come into a world governed by conformity to established standards and grow to mould ourselves into that standard. In negating the argument that the search for authenticity is culturally imposed, the existentialist perspective to authenticity poses this quest as an alternative to the normative in a world where what one does throughout his/her life has been done before, for example learning and working. Martin Heidegger asserts that we are lost in conformity and therefore stripped of our authenticity as a result. As one of the foremost existentialists, he suggests that the way out of this "lostness" is by facing what he calls our "ontological anxiety" – our fear and avoidance of the existential predicament of death. He proposes that "first we must acknowledge our ontological anxiety. This includes peeling away the protective evasions we have so cleverly woven to protect ourselves from the deepest truth of our being" (Heidegger, 2012). He further elaborates:

> *Once we have revived our ontological anxiety, we must keep it alive, not allow it to die away into comfortable obscurity once again. Instead of letting our being-towards-death fade back into the diversionary small talk of the 'they', we must focus our lives around this 'threat'. Then our ontological anxiety can become the light of our being—purifying, refining, & integrating our otherwise diffuse, preoccupied, & fragmented existence. In the light (or in the shadow) of this constant internal threat-to-being, we are empowered to choose our authentic projects-of-being—those basic endeavours that correlate best with our ontological anxiety.*

In essence, what Heidegger encourages us to reflect on is the inherent unifying truth to all our existence – that of impending death. Approaching life from this perspective of acknowledging and constantly revisiting our ontological anxiety therefore entices us to operate from a place of authenticity and alignment to our personal truths. However, Heidegger's concept of authenticity is not confounded by an either/or polarity where a person is either authentic or inauthentic. Rather, Heidegger posits that people achieve levels of authenticity in a process of becoming.

For Jean Paul Sartre, another renowned existential philosopher, authenticity is inextricably tied to exercising freedom. Sartre argued for the kind of freedom as he thought it to be inherent to making choices. In that freedom to explore and act upon the choices available, authenticity is expressed not only in having made the choice in alignment to a person's values but also in taking responsibility and ownership of the choices made. The antithesis to living an authentic life of freedom in his view is that of living in "bad faith" or *self*-deception (Weberman, 2011). Yet, unlike other definitions of the authentic *self* that is housed in finding the one true *self*, a Sartrean existentialist perspective entails that through the multitude of choices available to us, we become into being based on the freedom of choices we make.

"Authenticity is each human being's ability to fulfil his or her own potential and possibilities. To live authentically is to recognize that each hu-

man being is unique and to accept personal consequence that one has to find one's very own determination and realise one's own potential" ~ Mary Warnock

For Mary Warnock, authenticity is exemplified in the identification and manifestation of personal potential. Her concept of authenticity is a demonstration of how inherent to authentic living and being is the capacity of individuals to tap into and realize their personal abilities. In Warnock's approach, the notion of fulfilling personal potential therefore encompasses many of the other aspects to authenticity discussed above. Some examples are freedom, choice, ownership, truthfulness to *self*, social norm-defiance, *self*-expression and release.

In investigating a humanistic approach to authenticity, foremost humanistic psychology theorists Carl Rogers and Maslow view authentic persons through the lens of fully functioning or *self*-actualized persons. These are "Individuals who are born in tune with their basic nature and clearly and accurately see themselves and their lives. Because fully functioning persons are unencumbered by others' expectations for them, they can make more sound personal choices" (Avolio & Gardner, 2005). Such a humanistic perspective of authenticity ultimately is what the field of authentic leadership development is premised upon.

In summary, the following table formulated by Novicevic, Buckley, Brown, Harvey and Evans, reviews the various historical meanings assigned to authenticity by different thinkers.

Table 1: Historical Meanings of Authenticity (Brown, Evans, Buckely, Michael, & Novicevic, 2006, p. 66)

I. Philosophical Meanings
i. Authenticity as Moral Virtue
A moral response to declining civic and religious values (Baumaster, 1987).
One's emotional orientation toward the world (Furtak, 2003: 424).
The reflection of one's emotionally substantive way of living (Kierkegaard, 1996)
Virtuous aspiration to rise above the 'averageness' of following someone else's directions or following the crowd (Pianalato, 2003).
ii. Authenticity as Ethical Choices
Winning one*self*" by making authentic, *self*-motivated choices (Heidegger

1962/1927).
Recognition of one's psychological will and skill to balance private interest and public responsibility when choosing alternatives and setting goals (Sartre, 1948).
Capacity of the individual to search for progressive ways of harmonizing the demands of personal *self*-development with those of public responsibility to develop such capacity in others (Adorno, 1953).
Self as a difference between real and ideal mind and soul (Danzinger, 1997).
II. Psychological Meanings
iii. Authenticity as Trait/State
Individual-difference psychological construct that reflects not only *self*-awareness of one's motives and unbiased *self*-relevant cognitions, but also *self*-determination of one's behavioural and relational choices (Kernis, 2003a).
Expression of one's own convictions accompanied with the acceptance of responsibility for one's own decisions (Hoy et al., 1996).
Individual state that occurs when individuals *self*-regulate in ways that satisfy their basic psychological needs for competence, *self*-determination, and relatedness (Ryan & Deci, 2002).
Conflicting feelings and goals that meaningfully promoting *self*-growth experiences and informing about the complexity of one's true feelings (Goldman & Kernis, 2002:5).
iv. Authenticity as Identity
Meanings that we attach to our particular identities in *self*-referential terms Erickson (1995).
Owning one's personal "experiences" and acting in accord with one's inner thoughts and feelings (Harter, 2002).
Claim that is made by or for someone, thing, or performance and either accepted or rejected by relevant others (Peterson, 2005).
Individual judgment of his or her social roles using the norms that others would use to judge him or her.

3.2 Authentic Leadership

The concept of authenticity within leadership studies only began emerging in the latter half of the 20th century as philosophers started exploring the linkages between the two. As a newly emerging sub-field within leadership studies, a concept of leadership focusing on the various dimensions of a person's being is discussed through authentic leadership development.

For one of the earliest proponents of authentic leadership, R.B. Brumbaugh (1970), a leader's individual authenticity was strongly linked to an organization's authenticity (Brown, Evans, Buckely, Michael, & Novicevic, 2006, p. 68). Awareness of the *self*, *self*-worth and that of others was advocated as one of the hallmarks of authentic leadership, as championed as early as 1957 by Chris Argyris. Similarly, with the integrity of many leaders of large corporations and community leaders put into question in times of political and economic difficulty, the literature on authentic leadership is growing with consensus being built around how "evolving change requires leaders with a stable philosophy of the *self*, as well as of others in the organization and community (Brown, Evans, Buckely, Michael, & Novicevic, 2006, p. 65).

As the field of authentic leadership is a newly emerging field, there are many definitions of what constitute an authentic leader, depending on each proponent's school of thought. For Avolio, Luthans and Walumba, for example, an authentic leader exhibits a deep awareness of *self* and others. Concepts of confidence, hope, optimism and resilience are indicated to be the traits of authentic leaders (Avolio & Gardner, 2005, p. 321).

Shamir and Eilam posit that authentic leaders are governed by four characteristics that are similarly reflective of such an awareness of *self* as indicated by Avolio, Luthans and Walumba. These four characteristics are:

- A commitment to personal expectations rather than to that of others
- Motivation based on own established principles
- Non-imitation of others in their leaderships styles
- Action based on personal convictions and beliefs.

Offering a divergent view from the *self* as the centre of authentic leadership, Raymond T. Sparrowe explains what it means to be an authentic leader through the prism of hermeneutic philosophy, in which the *self* is characterized as a narrative project reflective of others. Whereas many proponents of authentic leadership like Avolio and others propose *self*-awareness as an internal process, Sparrowe posits that "others, then, are related to the *self* in two ways: first, as a source of imaginative variation in refiguring one's narrative identity and, second, as persons with whom our own histories are intertwined. Both imply a relationship in which others are constitutive of *self*hood as such" (Sparrow, 2005).

William L. Gardner, and others, put forth a model based on two key factors that support the development of authentic leadership: i. *self*-awareness of the leader which covers an understanding of his/her emotions, identity and values; and ii. *self*-regulation "including internalized regulation, balanced processing of information referring to the unbiased collection and interpretation of *self*-related information, authentic behaviour, and relational transparency which means that the leader displays high levels of openness, *self*-disclosure, and trust in close relationships" (Klenke, 2007).

For the purpose of this book, William L. Gardner's two-pronged *self*-based model of authentic leadership will be the basis for and prism through which the rest of the research discussion will ensue.

3.3 Developing authentic leaders

How can authentic leaders be developed? Is there a trusted method or formula through which authentic leadership is acquired? While most leadership skills are transferred in a training and seminar format, research on authentic leadership indicates that essential experiences of authentic leadership cannot be replicated in such environments (Shamir & Eilam, 2005). Shamir & Eilam propose ways of developing authentic leadership as follows:

> *One approach is to ask people to describe incidents involving their heroes and role models and explain why the behaviours are perceived as worthy of emulation. Another is to have people analyse their own experiences and ordeals to better understand their values and strengths. A more extreme approach is to provide opportunities to experience trigger events in which the need to overcome difficult challenges and crises will help people learn about their individual and shared values, beliefs, and competencies (Yukl, 2010).*

3.4 Linking peace to authentic leadership

Attaining and maintaining peace has been at the heart of human existence. Although as a field, the study of peace in academia is a recent phenomenon, people from all walks of life have grappled with notions of peace throughout history. Conceptions and interpretations of peace have been quite varied depending on the context in which it is being discussed and defined. Mostly understood as the absence of direct and structural violence inflicted across national and international stages, peace also extends to the interpersonal and personal realms of everyday existence. Given the plurality of peace definitions, this work adopts the understanding of many peace(s) in the Innsbruck School of Peace Studies tradition.

Weaving a peace perspective into this discussion is of great importance to my work because I hold the perspective that authenticity and *self*-transformation for leadership development are some of the key constructs to enabling and exercising peace in our daily lives. By condensing the analysis to the *self* as an authentic leader, my work posits that every individual is a leader and a peace practitioner, whether it is at the personal, interpersonal, community, national or international arena. Therefore, in looking at how transformative spaces enable authentic female leadership through *self*-transformation, my analysis is based on a trans-rational approach to peace.

3.5 Trans-rational Peaces

In the Innsbruck School of Peace Studies tradition, a five peace(s) model is considered as a response to the plurality of peace definitions that abound. The 'Five Peace Families' comprise an Energetic, Moral, Modern, Postmodern and Trans-rational interpretations of peace.

3.5.1 Energetic Peaces

An Energetic interpretation of peace is theorized to emerge out of harmonious relations between society, nature and the cosmos. The essence of this interpretation is in the perceived connection between everything as inherent to an expression of energy. Therefore, if everything is connected to everything else, then an understanding of peace in this context follows that peace begins in the innermost part of the *self* and proliferates all-round. An energetic interpretation of peace views the achievement of harmony through a unification of dualities – which means there is no absolute or ultimate truth based on constructed binaries of good vs bad; right vs wrong (Koppensteiner, 2010).

3.5.2 Moral Peaces

A moral perspective of peace is derived from a norm-based approach in which the notion of dualities is prominent. In the period of energetic peace(s), divinity was a virtue of all embodied in Mother Earth and energy perceived in its originary sense. The paradigm of moral peace(s), however, gives prominence to the presence of a personalized God that is omnipresent and omniscient. This God is external to the world, ever watchful and ever judging. Through this God is the norm of peace provided, followed and realized. These norms are dual in nature and subject to consequences if not adhered to, thereby facilitating the creation of norm based institutions (Koppensteiner, 2010).

3.5.3 Modern Peaces

In the modern tradition of peace, there is a movement away from God as the source of salvation towards the eminence of scientifically based truth as the absolute. As a result, the world and all its happenings from the perspective of modern peace can scientifically be determined. The notion of peace through God is converted in a sense towards peace through rationality (Koppensteiner, 2010). It is during this modern period that rationality paved for the conceptualization of the idealist and realist schools of thought and many other variations of modern peace, put forth by Hobbes, Rousseau, Kant and Marx (Dietrich).

3.5.4 Post-modern Peaces

The concept of many peace(s) begins to emerge in the post-modern thinking period, in which peace studies come to fruition as an academic discipline. There is a move away from the dichotomous notions of realism and idealism and a move towards harnessing a perpetual process of becoming towards peace. Generalizations and universalism is wholly rejected by way of deconstruction and the celebration of the multiplicity of existence and peace perspectives. The post-modern peace(s) perspective also marks the end of beliefs in certainties and evaluates so called facts within the prism of mere interpretations. Peace is therefore viewed as imperfect and humans both destined for cooperation and conflict. The crux of this thinking is therefore to acknowledge and accept both conflict and peace.

3.5.5 Trans-rational Peaces

The trans-rational approach to peace is transcendental in nature. It goes beyond the limits of modernity and post-modernity by including the energetic aspects of peace with the rational aspects of peace. This approach finds its roots in the humanistic, transpersonal and transhuman fields of psychology, acknowledging the transpersonal, systemic, ecological and spiritual dimensions of existence. In transcending modernity and post-modernity, rationality is not rejected. Rather is viewed as an element within the larger frame. In this regard, the distinction between mind and matter, between subject and object is not relevant anymore, as a trans-rational approach identifies and embraces the interconnectivity of people among each other and to nature as highly important. In acknowledging the subject as a whole, the task of the peace worker, therefore, is not to diagnose the process of peace as outside of him*self*/her*self*. More precisely, the task of the peace worker begins with work on the *self* (Koppensteiner, 2010).

As a personal worldview and for the purposes of this work, I adopt the trans-rational approach to peace in my discussions about enabling authentic leadership. As my work will look at the exercise of leadership by women in various spheres of their lives, the discussion will be guided by a trans-rational approach. By this I mean that facilitating leadership growth in people for the purposes of positively impacting their immediate and larger communities needs to be complemented by work on the *self* first. Therefore, the subject in the trans-rational tradition is not removed from the object. She, as the authentic leader, is connected with everything and everyone around her and in the process of becoming and being authentic, the *self* is taken as the first point of departure from which impacting for change and peace is conceivable.

As discussed in the various definitions of authenticity and recalling Sean Sayers's explanation in which authenticity entails identifying, understanding and acknowledging the various facets of the *self* for harmonious action, it can then be deduced that authenticity is a conduit for *becoming* into peace where a trans-rational approach to peace celebrates peace out of harmony.

~

CHAPTER FOUR

It is time to effect a revolution in female manners - time to restore to them their lost dignity - and make them, as a part of the human species, labour by reforming themselves to reform the world. It is time to separate unchangeable morals from local manners.
~ Mary Wollstonecraft

4. Culture & Her

4.1 Where is she a leader?

Looking into female leadership in Ethiopia as a whole, the discovery is that the sphere in which women can publicly influence and exercise their leadership is very marginal. Studies and reports draw a grim picture of female decision-making with many cultural and structural impediments at work. The role, however marginal, that women play in the public arena has not been documented. Even in current times, the curiosity and motivation by researchers to investigate this dimension is very slim. Historical accounts are dismal in their representation of women's agency and decision-making authority.

It is incredible that historians documenting the accounts of a country with more than two thousand years of history have left untapped and uncovered the wisdom and narrative of Ethiopia's female population. This omission may give the impression that a country graced with an indomitable historical landscape is loaded only with the tales and experiences of Kings, male warriors, heroes, saints and priests. Yet the few curious minds excavate, reveal and share a paradigm of Ethiopian women's historical engagement that is quite contrary to the silence, passivity and indifference with which historical texts and documents have treated them.

With the coming into power of a new government in 1992, what was in the preceding regime a marginally closed country began opening up to sign important legal instruments affirming the right of women and girls. Spaces opened up to include more women in public decision making and leadership roles and some government and civil society led campaigns on behavioural change towards gender sensitization began to take shape. A gradual change in politics and law enabling women to take up leadership positions ensued, yet not enough of the behavioural and attitudinal change to support women's changing roles. The stronghold that culture has on the attitude towards women's leadership by both men and women remains minimally challenged. Withstanding the structural limitations that impede women's public leadership capacities, this work focuses on a sub-set of the educated, female urbanites who already exercise some form of leadership within their homes, communities and as professionals in the work world.

There are an increasing number of women in professionalized sectors these days. The few educated Ethiopian women are increasingly exercising their leadership capacities in the public sector as civil servants; in the private sector as managers and deputy managers; and in the non-governmental sector as program managers and team leads. In their communities, women take a leading role within community associations formed around traditional forms of rotating credit associations (*Iqub)*, in burial societies (*Iddir)* and what may be religiously based or neighbourhood based associations (*Mahiber).* In their personal lives, women still maintain the traditional role of home-makers and care givers. While decision-making authority even within the home is hampered for the majority of Ethiopian women, the educated and professional few assume the double-burden of a full time professional life to come back to full time duties within the home.

Yet in a society in which the individual's behaviours and actions are predominantly driven by how one shows up to others and by keeping up appearances, the cultural weight of "how to be" is most heavily felt upon women. In such regard, I hold the point of view that women are limited from authentically expressing themselves and their leadership in the various facets of their lives if they continue to be swayed by cultural norms.

4.2 Norms that stifle growth

In researching women's and feminist leadership in Ethiopia, Indrawatie Biseswar points to various studies that identify the same obstacles faced by women in exercising leadership. Some of the ones of particular interest to this work are:

4.2.1 Cultural, traditional and religious belief systems

Although there are new emerging discussions that challenge cultural interpretations of a woman's appropriate place in society and what she can and cannot do, the notion of women as nurturers and caregivers concentrated in the homestead is upheld by a lot of women. Even as women attempt to challenge cultural norms, the inextricable link and intertwining of culture and religion makes it hard for women to unpack and deconstruct these cultural impositions. The majority of Ethiopians are staunch Christians, followed by Islamic tradition followers. Within the Christian grouping, while the majority is confined to the Ethiopian Orthodox Church traditions, many also follow the Evangelical protestant belief system.

As the dominant religious tradition in urban settings, Orthodox Christianity has many devout followers comprised of mostly female adherents. The weight of religious obedience is one that many women carry without challenging some of the norms that require female subservience and docility as prescribed by the Church (Biseswar, 2008). The concept of patience, tolerance and sacrifice is propagated to be a female virtue in the EOTC tradition. As a result, many devout female followers have grown into and through a system that has conditioned them from a young age towards accepting conformity and submissiveness as a characteristic that exemplifies female religious piety.

4.2.2 Socialization

The way in which Ethiopian women have been socialized from a young age has a great impact on how leadership is exercised. Embedded in a strong patriarchal culture, most men and a majority of women glorify male rationality deeming women as emotive beings lacking reason. By way of media proliferating gender stereotypical messages over a long period of time, the overall perception by women of themselves as capable and strong leaders is still in its infancy. To this day even the professional woman is pressured to conform to societal standards of homemaking as a prerequisite to reaching adulthood. The respect achieved by way of coming into marriage and childbirth far outweighs any leadership abilities exercised in any of the realms she negotiates. Therefore, much of the concern and energy expended is towards securing and maintaining such a contract.

4.2.3 Lack of confidence in women's capabilities

The prevailing mentality that women do not possess the capabilities necessary for leadership can be a stimuli for women to second guess their abilities if they are not strong minded and confident of their own skills. However, given the cultural impact in how women are socialized, the opportunities throughout their lives whereby they learn how to publicly exercise their leadership skills is often very limited. Not only in the passive games they are taught to play as young girls but also in the manner in which women at a young age are stripped of their critical analysis abilities where obedience to decisions made by parents primarily, but also by a male figure in the household is drilled early on (Zelelew).

4.2.4 Lack of assertiveness among women

Biseswar also cites the lack of assertiveness among Ethiopian women based on low *self*-esteem as another contributing factor that serves as an obstacle towards female leadership. The paradigm of patience, tolerance and sacrifice that is pushed on women often means that women lack the assertiveness in taking ownership of their lives and decisions. This is not to indicate that patience is not a virtue for change agents. As a peace disciple, I actually celebrate the notion of patience. Though not within the patriarchal context, in which I discuss the concept, where socialization and cultural indoctrination teaches women of sacrifice and men of assertiveness, creating the inevitable gender polarities.

4.3 Proverbs and their role in female representation

Amharic, a language of the Amhara ethnic group of northern Ethiopia and the official working language of the country, shapes to a great extent urban realities – specifically Addis Ababa. As one of the dominant cultures in the country channelling tradition through language, the use of Amharic proverbs is a common way of making statements in private and public life. Prominent women's rights activist, Meaza Ashenafi notes that,

> "proverbs of this area portray women as lacking wisdom, being irresponsible, adulterous, and only capable of domestic chores. Analysis of compiled proverbs shows that their objective is to sustain stereotypical gender-based roles that reinforce perceived credibility and wisdom of men the contrasting delicate emotional characteristics of women. These stereotypes contribute to women's inferior economic, social and political status. By extension, proverbs socialize both men and women to believe that men should play the public and political roles in society and women should be restricted to domestic chores (Ashenafi, 2009).

The use of proverbs as part of common patterns of communication is so ingrained so much so that even demeaning ones are taken for granted and as expressive of elderly wisdom. Women are also known to perpetuate the use of some of these proverbs, which are demeaning to women, without fully exploring the impact on shaping realities. Some of these proverbs often used are as follows:

- Do not trust the women

- The wisdom of a woman and the lights of stars do not take you far
- A woman and "toffa" (clay cooking pot) should be in the kitchen
- The companionship of a woman is dispersed by a mouse
- A chicken in the coop, a woman in the kitchen
- My mother plans for the day; my father, for the year
- A shy priest, a blind donkey and a courageous woman are useless
- Even if a woman has the knowledge, only a man can utilize his knowledge
- To talk is womanly and to work is manly
- A male where he is appointed, a female where she is married
- A woman's life is limited from the living room to the kitchen

The role that proverbs play in shaping and framing discourse driven realities is quite deep seated. Jeylan Wolyie Hussein in an analysis of the impact of such discourse posits that, "in principle, in a society structured along asymmetrical divisions, discourse, in addition to maintaining the asymmetrical relationship, has the power to persuade the subjugated to accept their own subjugation" (Hussein). In reference to this and in addition to some of the above-cited examples, proverbs seemingly facilitate a flawed space where women's value and contributions in society is not only doubted but also nullified. Such has been used to reinforce notions of disparity in ability between the sexes, further intensifying the cultural norms that stifle.

As a result, some of these demeaning proverbs are used by women in a reinforcement of portraying women as functional within the sphere of followership rather than leadership. Therefore the standards by which women are evaluated and assessed for their leadership is based on a masculine norm of reference. Consequently, the damage that culturally sanctioned proverbs cause as part of shaping reality and discourse is that women begin believing they cannot measure up accordingly.

4.3 Glass ceiling

Sometime in the 1980s Carol Hymowitz and Timothy D. Schellhardt coined the term *glass ceiling* to refer to the invisible barriers that hindered women from reaching the higher echelons of leadership in various sectors (Quast). Twenty years later the term is very much alive and in use to express the challenges women experience in climbing up the leadership ladder. As a global phenomenon, its effect is felt even much more in Ethiopia, were some of the cultural norms expressed previously, lend to making the Ethiopian glass ceiling ever more unbreakable.

The gendered division of roles in society is also glaringly reflected in organizations, where women take up the majority of administrative roles while men are relegated into the domain of authority and decision making. Meron Genene states that "even in occupations dominated by women such as the health field, when doctors and hospital heads are usually men while most nurses and support staff are women, men usually occupy the "more skilled", "responsible" and better-paid positions" (Genene, 2003). This reality is ever more pronounced even in everyday communication which is imbued with gendered language and reflecting the gender disparities. Some examples reflecting these stereotypes:

- A visit to a doctor's office results in a "I wanted to see him" (the doctor)
- Looking for a janitor leads to, "Call her" (the cleaner)
- In a situation requiring the intervention of a voice of authority, the request becomes, "who is he? Call him" (the manager)
- Looking for an office attendee, "Is she not in yet" (the receptionist)

These examples reflect an existing reality and a state of affairs leading many to assume that these roles are fixed and not interchangeable. The gendered language then becomes a product of a society's reality but in a cyclical manner, it also becomes responsible for creating and perpetuating such stereotypes.

While the limited number of highly educated women in addition to their domestic responsibilities may be explained as one of the reasons why women in Ethiopia do not climb the ladder faster, it is also not the norm for organizations in the country to put in place strategies and mechanisms that ensure women's steady climb up the ladder. A former female member of government explains that during her years working in a specific Ministry, she was one among a handful of women slowly climbing up the ladder in a male dominated industry. She shares that she and her other female colleagues were trying to survive in a "house made only for men". She points to the lack of a support system encouraging women to advance further. As well that the system is designed not with women's needs to succeed in mind. In her analysis, she does not blame anyone, stating that the men do not understand what it takes to include women in their world and that women lack awareness and training to demand their needs. Her suggested remedy to the glass ceiling is the need for a systemic change and a paradigm shift to reach parity.

A highly passive approach by women in claiming leadership roles and tasks is attributable to the lack of assertiveness and lack of confidence displayed. Additionally the double burden of a professional life and responsibilities assumed in the domestic sphere limit women from navigating networking opportunities that exist. These informal platforms are where most often a variety of opportunities abound but which women are not adequately tapping into as a result of their commitments to the homestead. The glass ceiling therefore remains ever more firm and unbreakable since women are not positioning themselves to be visible in terms of the skills and potential they possess.

4.4 Feedback from Ethiopian women

To get a sense of other women's perspective on culture, women and leadership in Ethiopia, I sought the input of professionals who are in various stages of positional leadership within their careers. The questions I posed to them and their responses are not to be taken as conclusive and representative in its analysis of authentic female leadership in Ethiopia. Rather, the purpose is to identify some of the issues that are at play when referring to women's expression of leadership in the country. I shared the questionnaire to thirty-five women of which only ten responded and therefore I have chosen to share their perspective in an attempt to shed light on some of the experiences.

The following seven questions were compiled and posed to the respondents:

1. How do you define authenticity?
2. How do you define leadership?
3. Which characteristics do you think Ethiopian women need to be authentic leaders?
4. What cultural factors do you think support personal leadership among women in Ethiopia?
5. What cultural factors do you think obstruct personal leadership among women in Ethiopia?
6. What do you think is essential in fostering personal leadership abilities among Ethiopian women? (please be specific)
7. Where and how do you think women can foster such abilities?

Here below is a compilation of the responses provided by the respondents:

4.4.1 Respondent 1

Authenticity is facing your fears and consistently weeding it out. Leadership is Courage. To be authentic leaders, Ethiopian women need honesty about who they are and honesty about what they want. A strong national identity supported by thousands of years of history, bravery and patriotism are some of the cultural factors that support personal leadership among women in Ethiopia. Whereas, machismo, religious teachings, the lack of a culture of self-reflection, self-appreciation and the foreignness of the concept of self-worth and taking stock of one's strengths are some of the cultural factors that obstruct personal leadership among women in Ethiopia.

The courage to take responsibility for their position in life; the courage to dare and be different; to defy the norm and to let go of looking good and to let go of the need to be liked; to be generous and share, to teach and the desire to learn from each other is essential in fostering personal leadership abilities among Ethiopian women. Women can foster such abilities in a circle of supporting and nurturing environment such as AWiB. Additionally, their desire for continuous learning, curiosity, self-discipline and a burning desire for education can support the growth of such abilities as a learned society is self-led.

4.4.2 Respondent 2

Authenticity is a defining trait of leaders. It is a high level of candour, when we communicate openly, share our thoughts and feelings and mean what we say. It is an alignment between what we think, say and do. Also being the self, and owning the different parts of the self that we often disassociate from – the fearful self, the angry self, the needy self, etc. I like this quote: "The main ingredient in rapport is authenticity. The more you surrender to who you are in front of others the more at home they will feel." --- Chip Bell ---

Leadership is 'Thinking, listening, speaking and acting in a way that mobilizes the self and others into effective action, for the creation of a new future'. To be authentic leaders Ethiopian women need to act beyond their fear, transcending cultural expectations, speaking up and out on issues that matter, and recognizing their essence and power.

I think the collectivist way of thinking – our sense of identity related to others supports personal leadership among women in Ethiopia. We live Ubuntu – we are because others are, so we pay attention to reaching out for others when they need support. We often put others first, so we are ready and open to serve. According to many people who come from abroad, and compared to other African countries, we are still open and thirsty to learn. We have the humility to do so. And we are also inclined to 'speak less' and act more – this is subject to perception though.

However, the expectations on the role of women – to be quiet, subservient, accepting, confined to domestic roles, and expected to maintain harmony – not 'embarrassing' others by engaging in conflict or expressing one's views, serves to obstruct personal leadership in women. The following can be utilized to foster personal leadership abilities among Ethiopian women:

- *Create spaces for women to reflect on the self and one's strengths and potential*
- *Develop individual agency, will, initiative and freedom to create in the face of resignation and negative circumstances.*
- *Foster ability to exercise critical thinking about self and society.*
- *Competencies in self and social awareness and management (Emotional Intelligence).*
- *The ability to think, speak and listen to inspire and mobilize others into effective action*
- *Competencies in designing and delivering on breakthrough actions that can benefit the self and society*
- *The capacity to collaborate with like-minded people, beyond just having a spirit of competition*

The above are inspired by my work on Leadership Development.

Women can foster such abilities through practice, acting because of, and in spite of fear, and spending company with like-minded people who can support and inspire them. I also feel that when we declare a new possibility and act to make that breakthrough happen, we learn in action, and thus grow.

4.4.3 Respondent 3

I am not sure of how to define authenticity. Leadership for me is sharing and empowering. When you are able to share your time knowledge even your attention with your co-workers, partners etc. Empowering means giving them the space to be creative and giving them your guidance by sharing your experience and time, as well as giving the opportunity to be part of the decision making processes. The characteristics that Ethiopian women need to be authentic leaders are humility, confidence, honesty, the ability to be articulate, and knowledge of what her rights are. As it relates to what cultural factors support women's leadership, different cultures have different ways of supporting women's leadership but I am afraid the opposite is greater than the positive sides of it. The fact that from childhood girls and boys are given different roles in the society starting from the toy they play with are cultural factors that hinder women's personal leadership. I know there are different theories associated to this but generally speaking, women are expected to be caretakers of the house as men are the stronger mostly the decision makers in most places.

To foster personal leadership among women in the country, building confidence mainly through education, trainings etc, exposing them to different books, encouraging them to read more, exposing them to stories of successful women within the same cultural settings is essential. Seeing the kind of life most women lead, struggling day to day, it may be thought of as luxurious in fostering personal leadership, but there are always less expensive ways of reaching to a majority by using local settings like idirs, small microfinance associations, etc.

4.4.4 Respondent 4

Authenticity is all about intentions. There are many things we say or do with the full intention that they create an ambiguous outcome so that we can say later that that's not what we meant to say or do. The authentic words or actions are those that are brave enough to be unambiguous and to arise out of noble intentions.

Rather than mere management, leadership has the elements of inspiration and vision-setting. A leader is necessarily courageous and she's able to see the big picture rather than 'sweat the small stuff.' Good leaders have at least an element of charisma and they're able to get others excited about their project and methods. Characteristics of authentic leadership for women comprises the courage to speak up, admit mistakes and make unpopular decisions; recognition that a good leader doesn't please everybody; consistency; honesty; fairness; consideration for others and genuine encouragement of other women.

The cultural factors supporting women's leadership include strong family and community networks and a tradition of hiring house help and childcare, both of which enable educated women to work and excel outside the home. Respect for age, experience and formal qualifications, which ensure that at least some women get ahead. While the cultural factors obstructing women's leadership include deep-rooted sexism which is not problematized by women and men and which pulls down women. Relatedly, women's lack of confidence and fear of displeasing subordinates affect women's leadership.

In order to foster Ethiopian women's leadership we need formal and informal women-focused, on-the-job applicable trainings. A mentorship system for more mature women leaders to support younger women would also create a more sustainable pool of women leaders. Women can foster these abilities at the workplace and in their personal lives through personal commitment to be, support and learn from women leaders. Wherever possible, women should initiate informal and formal networks whereby they can learn from and support other women leaders and mentor younger women.

4.4.5 Respondent 5

I would define authenticity as being aware of oneself, others and circumstances around and remaining true to self in relation to surroundings. Authenticity connotes integrity for one can be authentic when her inside and outside world match and can be herself without masks. It is self-awareness and being oneself, which can be demonstrated to others powerfully.

Leadership is a purpose driven concept that takes people from one stage to another with the value of excellence, establishing good relationship, and imparting vision to accomplish the common purpose.

The characteristics women need to be authentic are knowledge of circumstances, context and surroundings. However, I see a gap in self-knowledge and conducting oneself confidently.

Cultural factors that support women's personal leadership: Women are expected to manage their home and children. A person who does not know how to manage her life is not in a better position to lead the family's life. Women's social role is also appreciated culturally. So a person who does not care about herself cannot be a model for society. Women's caring role can be taught it all starts with self-care: physically, mentally, emotionally, spiritually and socially. So the focus of others can be reversed that the starting point is the SELF.

Cultural factors that obstruct women's personal leadership: Talking from the Addis Ababa city life perspective, women are expected to fulfil all the triple roles of reproductive, productive and social ones. Women have to make money to support to the family and kids needs supporting the husband. Women have to take care of husband and children's needs. Women are expected to get married soon and make babies to fulfil the social roles. These days, we find many unfulfilled women due to advancing in one and "lagging behind" in another. So the society's expectation puts a lot of pressure on professional or business-women but who are not married and do not have children.

To foster personal leadership abilities among Ethiopian women the following are essential:

- *Providing a forum whereby women can discuss life issues.*
- *Providing different trainings that enhance personal awareness and development.*
- *Availing economic empowerment opportunities to free herself to think above basic needs.*
- *Availing educational opportunities.*

Women can foster such abilities by being conscious of oneself and others and circumstances and grabbing all opportunities for self-development. It can never be easy for women so knowing that and developing resilience is important to fit in this society.

4.4.6 Respondent 6

Authenticity is all about finding out who we really are and what we stand for; digging deep inside us to find what moves us, what are our beliefs. My definition of leadership is - the ability to socially influence others in order to get their support and commitment to accomplish a common task. This implies an acceptance of the person by others as s/he is able to affect emotions, opinions, or behaviours of others.

Characteristics I think Ethiopian women need to be "authentic" leaders is to understand the link between authenticity and leadership as a start. If we as leaders can be authentic we would be able to build and sustain trust with others through real relationships, stand for what you feel is right and important and not seek others approval as most women leaders here in Ethiopia do - do what we say without exception. Most important of all "stop making excuses" –

if you want to be a leader get out and earn it – network, read, participate in leadership sessions, have mentors etc.

I divide cultural factors I think obstruct personal leadership into two – internal and external. Internal or personal factors are:

- *Women not seeing themselves out in the professional arena*
- *Not taking the initiative to excel – women are comfortable in handling easy tasks which does not require them to give in extra*
- *Not believing in ourselves – we think success is for MEN*

External factors are:

- *Cultural factor – women's role is viewed as being a domestic – daughter who fetches the water, cooks etc., or a mother who needs to take care of kids and husband etc.*
- *Economic factor – as a result of their marginalized roles women are not financially better off to invest back on their career development*

To foster personal leadership abilities among Ethiopian women I think networking, having mentors, continued education and exposure to other countries is important. Women can foster these abilities by:

- *Being part of professional networks to have visibility and share experience*
- *By having a clearly defined career goal and asking where does each job I take fit in my future career goal*
- *Taking courses, classes – online as well as taking part in various trainings and workshops organized in and out of country*
- *Make reading a culture*

4.4.7 Respondent 7

Authenticity is being and/or staying true to self. Ethiopian women need to be educated, fearless and free to be "authentic" leaders. Our subtle culture of tactfulness – the distinct ability to talk our way through is a cultural factor supporting personal leadership. Yet, our mind-boggling rush to settle (in every sense of the word) is a cultural factor that I think obstructs personal leadership among women in Ethiopia. By re-learning how to dream bigger and better personal leadership abilities can be fostered among us. Women can foster such abilities by consciously choosing to live, learn and contribute everywhere as you learn and live everywhere.

4.4.8 Respondent 8

Authenticity for me is always attached to living a life of consciousness at all times. It means always having integrity no matter what you do and making sure all our actions reflect our purpose and what we stand for. Leadership is inspiring others enough to repeat what the leader does. Not what the leader says but what the leader does.

To be "authentic" leaders, I think Ethiopian women need education, integrity, self-awareness and self-confidence. In terms of cultural factors supporting personal leadership, to be honest, I can't think of any. I think the cultural practices have always encouraged women to be ardent followers of men. Although it's hard to generalize on this fact, almost all successful women leaders that I know earned their position in society by defying the cultural expectations the society has imposed on them. They all gravitated towards non-conformity in their own rights tenaciously saying 'No' to condescending social norms. Sadly, as a member of the younger generation of future women leaders, I had to fight for what I believe in. I had to prove myself to be accepted for thinking differently than the generations before me. I wonder how long we have to go through the same path before our culture evolves to support women not just as domesticated homemakers and mothers but as leaders and business owners. In most cases our women are held back from achieving their professional goals or reaching their potential due to social conventions, gender inequality, peer pressure and familial expectations, all directly or indirectly tied to our cultural and religious background and the conservative ways by which parents raise their children.

Training, self discipline, lifelong learning and most importantly education are key factors in fostering personal leadership abilities among women. I'm a firm believer that despite limited educational opportunities and stifling cultural norms, women should always chase after their dreams aggressively. Especially in a country like ours where gender inequality hinders a woman's role and meaningful participation in society.

In my view there's no specific place where women (or men) can adopt lifelong learning. As an aspiring Ethiopian woman, lifelong learning, to me, means always keeping an open mind and learning from every little experience, life lessons, observations and even mistakes despite the limitations that we face or the limited resources and opportunities available to us. The US millionaire and business tycoon Mark Cuban coined the term ABL (Always Be Learning) to stress on the importance of being in a constant mode of learning whether or not you're successful, educated, and rich or still getting there. The point for me is to always be mindful of personal growth, expanding potential and reaching for higher limits by learning from our environment, our interactions and our experiences. It has to do with always being ready for improvement and applying what we've learned in our day-to-day lives.

4.4.9 Respondent 9

Authenticity is a person's ability to stay true for himself/herself. This can be reflected in the consistent patters the person follows throughout his/her life.

Leadership is the ability of one to lead self after being able to gain a sense of balance in his/her life. This leader who has gained balance can be an example for many others to learn and grow.

To be "authentic" leaders, Ethiopian women need the following characteristics:

- *Commitment*
- *Confidence*
- *Truthfulness*
- *Integrity*
- *Dreamers*
- *Hopeful*
- *Passionate to give service and more focused on others than self*
- *Know the value of love*

Having the culture of great social support is a great advantage that supports women to appropriate time for needs of personal development. As it relates to cultural factors obstructing personal leadership, generally speaking, the existence of a patriarchal society that only supports men's personal development as leaders, gender socialization that facilitates leadership roles for men, violence and disproportionate cultural provisions of opportunities for men are few of the obstacles that women face. To foster personal leadership abilities bringing gender equality through gender mainstreaming as well as having relevant affirmative measures when it is so required to compensate past historical disadvantages is necessary. Women can also foster leadership abilities through formal or informal learning such as education institutions, through women's networking platforms (through membership or volunteerism), trainings, etc.

4.4.10 Respondent 10

Authenticity is being self, living the reality, and avoiding fear of what people say about others or me. Leadership is influencing others, being a role model and empowering others.

As Ethiopian women we need to be bold enough to address our issues. We need to be assertive and proactive. We have to take initiatives to change ourselves and other women. We need to be visible. The socialization and networking help as cultural factors supporting leadership. We are not individualists so that we can use our social network to grow/demonstrate our personal leadership.

However, our culture also discourages women to be open to public or to take opportunities to address their issues openly. E.g. we don't speak our ideas openly or freely in fear of what others say about us. To foster leadership abilities women need to be bold enough to ask, know, learn, speak out, etc.

Women can foster leadership abilities starting from home to offices, at social gatherings and any networking events like AWiB, Toastmasters and other professional gatherings. It is also good to have informal women group in places like at gym, hairdresser, etc.

4.5 Where can she become a leader?

We are in a period of economic transformation that is greatly triggering social transformation. Female breadwinners abound tasked with a professional life and the double-burden of being a home caretaker. Nevertheless, as industries expand throughout the country, the opportunities for women to play a greater role in the public sphere are also increasing. However, the chances for women's greater visibility still remain untapped in both the private and public sectors.

Indrawatie Biseswar argues that educated Ethiopian women have fallen behind in not only cultivating leadership aspirations but also in acting upon them. She emphasizes that there are quite a lot of educated and exposed women who can play a meaningful role in providing leadership but fail to do so. She continues to argue that:

> *Many simply have never considered that option and leave it to "others", including outsiders and foreigners. This in turn contributes to the lack of local initiatives in the field. The almost indestructible cultural stereotypes add more weight to this inaction. And, though one can be assured that stereotypes can be overcome through education, when it concerns women's leadership in Ethiopia, education plays no role in influencing people's thoughts* (Biseswar, 2011).

Whereas cultural norms continue to shape the manner in which women traverse the public sphere, the educated female minority are now tasked with the responsibility of paying it forward. This means, where walking through the doors to advance further in their careers may not be a choice for some, it remains that there are opportunities for women to exercise their leadership in a variety of ways.

4.5.1 Educators

The educated minority can play a leading role in sharing and disseminating their knowledge either at a personal level, at an organizational or even public level. The creative methods of doing this are abundant and serve as a form of exercising their leadership through experience and knowledge sharing and exchange. I.e. writing, blogging, public speaking, etc. I was recently asked to share some of the core concepts of Non-violent communication as a means of conflict transformation for an online radio station which is aired in up to six countries including Ethiopia. The owner of the station who also happened to be the interviewer expressed to me that I am the first Ethiopian female who agreed to her request for an interview. This shows that there is reluctance by way of fear or shyness expressed by Ethiopian women in sharing the knowledge and experience they have.

Similarly, one of the concept drivers of a book project focused on Ethiopian Women of Accomplishment recently mentioned to me that there is a generation of women in Ethiopia who have first-hand experience of the Derg regime and currently in Addis Ababa but who have declined several request for interviews of their active roles of leadership through that period in history.[2]

4.5.2 Activists & Advocates

Given the privileged position educated women find themselves in they have the space and means to be able to advocate and champion for a number of social and political issues in the country. While the realm of politics in Ethiopia is a complicated space tantamount to duress, the need for much stronger female voices is apparent. With very little female representation in politics, and one that is mired by tokenism and party loyalty (Biseswar, 2011), an educated Ethiopian woman must test the grounds and exercise her authentic leadership capacities in this domain.

4.5.3 Mentors

The role mentors play in the professional and personal development of any person – male or female – is highly researched and documented. The practice of female mentorship in Ethiopia however is very limited. Such is another area in which educated and experienced women in the country can exercise leadership by serving as mentors to young up and coming professionals. The provision of guidance to young women in negotiating the complexities of a

---

2 The Derg Regime was the military junta that deposed the last Emperor of Ethiopian in 1974 and ruled by terror until its overthrow in 1991. Given the limited documentation of Ethiopian women's role in history, the few that survived the atrocities committed in during that period have been approached to share their stories as part of a book project which intends to capture the stories of many women in the country. The book thereafter is intended for distribution throughout the country with the aim of provided young women stories of women who blazed trails ahead of them.

transforming society cannot be understated. The few women in visible positions of leadership that share their stories all point to a mentor who had coached them into growth. Therefore, a form of exercising leadership is governed and measured by the extent to which an individual is readily disposed to supporting the advancement and movement of a mentee.

4.5.4 Role models

The discussion on mentorship brings to point a highly pertinent issue which is coming to the fore in very recent times in the country. This is the issue of female role models. The norm thus far has been for young females to look up to women who are far out of reach to their respective realities. Many young women who are asked who their role models are point to either their immediate family – their mother – or are externally referenced; often quoting the names of Western female movie and song stars. This is clearly evident of a deficit of information on leading female personalities and leaders in the country.

A growing body of research suggests that strong same-sex role models are especially important for the personal and professional development of young women and girls. Role models are highly important in communities; they are concrete examples that people in our society who share important elements of our identity are achieving success. Role models in sharing their stories and the journey of their success offer hope to those who may have experienced similar circumstances. They offer inspiration to those who have wanted to set foot on a specific path but have limited information on how to proceed. Role models provide confirmation that the path to success is not predetermined and uniform. Rather they indicate that there is a plethora of approaches to leading our lives remarkably with purpose and impact. Therefore, women who have defied culturally sanctioned challenges have the potential to inspire young women and girls in the country to become better versions of themselves, by serving as positive role models.

Drawing upon an example at a grassroots level, about two years ago I conducted a focused group discussion with in school and out of school rural community girls in a research exercise aimed at gauging their media savvy. The exercise consisted of showing these girls and their community gatekeepers' short videos produced of young women coming from very humble origins that had created a means of livelihood and were excelling. The profundity of that exercise still strikes me to this day in the sense that the young girls watching the videos were in total awe and amazement at how their peers had surpassed various obstacles to create personal possibilities.

The urban young I shared the question of role model importance with expressed that having an Ethiopian woman as a role model was important to them for the following reasons:

> *"It's always good to have someone that you can really relate to. I mean there might be people that you admire and consider as your role models in the world, yet having someone that you can look up to who is Ethiopian - you share the same culture and tradition, same history - it does increase the level of confidence you have."*
>
> *"Because you know if someone you know who is near you can do it, you can also do it."*
>
> *"It enables you to imagine of better things within the same context and how socially defined parameters can be overcome"*
>
> *"As we come from the same environment and live among same society we will experience the same obstacles and it helps us to figure out how to live our life in the best way we can"*
>
> *"Because it teaches us that there is nothing which is not achievable as they are already achieving it"*

In this light, some of what AWiB aims to do is make visible the work of great women leaders in the nation so that a generation of younger women can look up to some of them as role models to emulate. From the monthly programs hosted to the information on the life and work of various women that we disseminate, the feedback generated from various women in all walks of life is how they have been moved by the stories that are being shared and how they are inspired for action as well.

Many of the movies, dramas and advertisements in the country do nothing to place women in positions of leadership. More than print materials, radio and TV have far better reach to women in the country. However, the movies and radio dramas presented for public consumption do very little to challenge the culturally sanctioned gender norms in the country. Women who have achieved great success in their endeavours are not made visible as needs be to support the impact of their work on other aspirants. Both Biseswar and Genene point to the lack of information on female role models in the country as one of the factors that inhibit women's leadership capacity enhancement in the country.

In conclusion, it is important to note that part of the endeavour of exercising authentic leadership by women in the country is inextricably linked to challenging cultural norms that stifle such expressions of leadership in the country. Linked to the discussion of role modelling, the few women in the country who go against traditional norms are crucial to mobilizing the curiosity and activity of other educated Ethiopian women. This is to create a ripple effect that not only permeates the elite and privileged within the country, but also transcends and trickles down to the grassroots level. In the next chapter, the very essence of what *self*-transformation for authentic leadership means is discussed at length.

CHAPTER FIVE

Any transition serious enough to alter your definition of self will require not just small adjustments in your way of living and thinking but a full-on metamorphosis.
~ Martha Beck

5. The Transformational *Self*

5.1 *Self*-Transformation

The various literatures on authentic leadership indicate that authenticity is rooted in the notion of a *true self*. Donna Ladkin and Steven S. Taylor accept this aspect of a *true self* but argue that it is the way in which this *true self* is enacted which is critical to followers' experience of authentic leadership (Ladkin & Taylor, 2010). An interpretation of their argument of enactment, introduces the perspective of a transformation that needs to occur in bringing forth the *true self* which is assumed to not be fully in place yet in the aspiration to become an authentic leader. Transformation then becomes a process of uprooting what is thought to be the only way of being and transforming towards a complete paradigm shift in which the manner of thought, speech, behaviour and relating to *self* and others changes to better serve our needs.

The fascination with *self*-transformation is not exclusive to our current society. From ancient times, the quest for personal understanding and transformation has been a quest that has infiltrated an individual's spiritual and secular journey. Various spiritual traditions are imbued with a concept of transformation in which the *self* is understood to better serve its purpose and others once it has gone through a process of shedding what is considered by *self* as its "ills".

In the discussion within this work, transformation is closely linked to the concept of *self*-actualization as studied and explained through humanistic psychology. Where the discussion of enabling female authentic leadership is examined through the prism of realizing one's full potential, transformation is therefore seen in this work as a process through which one's *self*-actualization needs are met. In Abraham Maslow's definition of *self*-actualization, the driving force is the realization and development of one's personal capacities. He states that *self*-actualization, "refers to our desire for *self*-fulfilment, namely, to the tendency for a person to become actualized in what he or she is potentially . . . the desire to become more and more what one is, to become everything that one is capable of becoming . . . what one can be, one must be" (Hunt).

This actualizing, transforming or becoming into the true *self* imagines an embracement of one*self*, others and the process of living as opposed to existing in constant rivalry to the needs of the true *self*. Richard Bach captures the sentiment of transformation in the following quote: "*What the caterpillar calls the end of the world. The master calls a butterfly.*" This quotation epitomizes an evolutionary process of a new life emerging from the old and becomes symbolic of the materialization of the true *self* long shrouded under the guise of norms. However, is *self*-transformation an evolutionary process that bids its time and happens or can it be a *self*-initiated process?

The various phases of life and experiences trigger a cycle of evolution that the *self* undergoes. These can come in the form of deep trigger events and can constitute anything from the loss of a loved one to unexpected and unsettling experiences encountered in daily living or positive experiences which have the effect of stretching one beyond their comfort zones. Transformation can also be *self* driven or initiated in the sense that an individual senses or becomes conscious of an aspect of *self* that he/she wants to change and therefore begins taking the steps towards the transformation sought.

5.2 The Evolving *Self*

This notion of an evolving *self* is well captured is Robert Kegan's constructive-developmental model of the constitutions of the *self*, in which he categorizes people spiralling through five distinct orders of the developing *self* (Berger). Kegan places the majority of adults in the third order – the socialized or traditional mind. To explain a bit more about the transition of the *self* in this evolution:

5.2.1 First Order – The Impulsive balance

In the First Order, where Kegan places most young children, the notion of "durable objects" or the idea of an unchanging quality of things in the world, is brought into perspective. Rules are made not to be broken and the complexity of opinions is not yet fully realized and understood. A caretaker's role is quite pronounced here, as children in this Order need to be reminded time and again of the rules in place. Therefore, the opinions and worldview of the caretaker *self* is instilled in the young child as codified law by which he/she must abide for survival.

5.2.2 Second Order – The Imperial balance

The discovery of feelings and beliefs that remain constant over time is the discovery of the "Sovereign" mind or Second Order in Kegan's model. He relegates older children and adolescents into this tier, where "children –and adults- at this stage are *self*-centred and see others as helpers or barriers on the road to get their desires" (Berger). The *self* in this order is supervised. Where a rule is adhered to it is in fear of reprisal or punishment and where it becomes an obstacle, the possibility for a way out with minimal damage is sought.

5.3.3 Third Order – The Interpersonal balance

The "Socialized" or "Traditional" mind referred to earlier where Kegan places a majority of adults is where we begin to witness the concepts of cultural norm attribution. Third Order minds have evolved to navigating abstract thoughts and are *self*-reflective. However, there is a tendency to ascribe to the expectations of others and adherence to social roles established. As Kegan puts it, this *self* in this stage is not independent of the context of "other people liking". "When I live in this balance as an adult I am the prime candidate for the assertiveness trainer, who may tell me that I need to learn how to stand up for my*self*, be more "*self*ish," less pliable, and so on, as if there were mere skills to be added on to whoever else I am" (Kegan, 1982). What this means is that individuals in the interpersonal balance stage of evolution cannot fathom the concept of *self*-esteem where such is referenced and derived in reflection of others. A third Order mind contextualized in reflection of his/her environment and social reference points can only begin speaking of concepts like *self*-esteem and confidence when he/she evolves out of dependence on norm adherence.

5.3.4 Fourth Order – The Institutional balance

Kegan's transformation of the *self* from the third order of interpersonal balance to the fourth order of institutional balance is characterized by *self*-authorship, independence and expressed autonomy. The individual in this stage of evolution occupies the realm of "I have relationships" in sharp contrast to the third Order definer of "I am my relationships" (Kegan, 1982). The opinions and ideas of others upon which the *self* was highly reliant and dependent upon begin to dissipate and are replaced by an internal and very personal set of rules and regulations. "The institutional balance does not leave one bereft of interpersonal relationships, but it does appropriate them to the new context of their place in the maintenance of a personal *self*-system" (Kegan, 1982).

5.3.5 Fifth Order – The Interindividual balance

According to Kegan, only small subsets of adults find themselves transformed into the fifth Order, where recognition of the plurality of selves within the *self* is acknowledged. The move from subject orientation to object specificity is somewhat reached at this stage, thereby broadening the perspective and scope of the individual's complex social world. Objectivity is not totally achieved per se, but at this level, the *self* is less identified to subjective conceptions and institutional identification with the *self*. Kegan explains,

> *If one no longer is one's institution, neither is one any longer the duties, performances, work roles, career which institutionality gives rise to. One has a career; one no longer is a career. The self is no longer so vulnerable to the kind of ultimate humiliation which the threat of performance-failure holds out, for the performance is no longer ultimate....the self seems available to "hear" negative reports about its activities; before, it was those activities and therefore literally "irritable" in the face of those reports. Every new balance represents a capacity to listen to what before one could only hear irritably, and the capacity to hear irritably what before one could hear not at all. But the increased capacity of the stage 5 balance to hear, and to seek out, information which might cause the self to alter its behaviour, or share in a negative judgement of that behaviour, is but a part of that wider transformation which makes stage 5 capable, as was no previous balance, of intimacy.*

In Kegan's model, the interindividual balance is also known as the *self*-transforming mind. This *self*-transforming mind has the ability to go beyond the *self* and observe it*self* objectively, bringing into awareness the evolutionary and transcendental aspect of life where anything given is not permanent but under a state of constant flux. This state of constant flux is not treated as a destabilizing effect on the *self*. Rather the interindividual balance *self* perceives this as an opportunity to revisit and understand tensions between different values, ideologies and systems as they arise.

In disassociating from the constructions of the *self*, the interindividual balance *self* is highly disposed to building intimacy in all sorts of relationships. "This intimacy is, for the first time, the *self's* aim rather than its source" (Cairn). As Kegan explains, the capacity of the *self* in the interindividual balance stage of development, for enabling intimacy emerges from its own capacity to be intimate with itself. Hence the capacity to share itself with others. "This sharing of the *self* at the level of intimacy permits the emotions and impulses to live in the intersection of systems, to be "re-solved" between one *self*-system and another. Rather than the attempt to be both close and auto-regulative, "individuality" permits one to "give oneself up" to another; to find oneself in what Erikson has called "a counter-pointing of identities" (Kegan, The Constitutions of the Self).

The interindividual balance stage of the *self* can then presumably be equated with an authentic *self* that transcends conceptions of identity that have been culturally imposed. The move away from the subjective orientation of the *self* to an objective appeal liberates the *self* towards an authentic representation of itself as defined in Chapter 3. While according to Kegan's model, the fifth order is the enlightened stage of human conscious development; the fourth order where *self*-authorship and autonomy are expressed can also be viewed as the stage where authenticity begins to develop.

In the third order, meaning derived from how others see and experience the *self* is the guiding principle for how one conducts himself/herself. Such a disposition may raise the propensity to be less authentic in exercising leadership according to the conceptions of autonomy and remaining true to *self* as discussed in previous chapters. Although like Kegan, this work takes the perspective that being in the third order is not a "bad" thing per se, it also takes the approach of an impending evolution that is needed to enable the unleashing of authenticity in how leadership is exercised. The following section discusses four elements this work has chosen to constitute a transformation of the self for authentic leadership.

5.3 Transforming to the "Authentic *Self*"

5.3.1 *Self*-awareness

"*Self*-awareness is the pivot point on which your leadership depends…without it, your orientation to your true north is missing," states Bill George as a testament to the necessity of understanding the inclinations and motivations of the *self* or knowing "what is under the hood." The concept of *self*-awareness is considered one of the key pillars to developing the *self* as an authentic leader. Many descriptions and definitions of *self*-awareness point towards possessing emotional intelligence or the ability to observe and scrutinize one's own feelings and that of others towards utilizing the information to guide one's behaviours and actions (Condon, 2011). Recent research argues in favour of including knowledge of one's cognitive abilities and social intelligence as part of the *self*-aware individual. However, for the purposes of this work, *self*-awareness will be addressed in close connection to Daniel Goleman's theorizing of emotional intelligence (EI) as it encompasses a *self*-dimension that is highly cognizant and aware of interpersonal abilities that are required in responding to others.

"*Self*-awareness means having a deep understanding of one's emotions, strengths, weaknesses, needs and drives. People with strong *self*-awareness are neither overly critical nor unrealistically hopeful. Rather, they are honest – with themselves and with others" (Goleman, 2004). Therefore, becoming an authentic leader entails developing a sense of *self*-awareness as part of the transformative process of the *self* whereby one possesses and understanding of how personal feelings can affect the environment in which one is in. Such a heightened sense of awareness of the *self* and how the *self* relates to the external environment is crucial to the ability to transform dynamics of the external environment that has presented it*self* as non-conducive to a thriving *self*.

A second dimension of *self*-awareness is tied to an understanding of personal values and goals. A thorough appreciation of one's values and goals means that the *self* is neither distracted nor tempted by short-term enticements which are not in alignment with the goals and values set by the *self*. The *self*-aware authentic leader is therefore driven by a values based compass which guides him/her according to short-term or long-term goals that have been set personally rather than socially (Goleman, 2004).

Goleman also posits that confidence is another hallmark of the *self*-aware individual. This confidence is exhibited in a comfort to talk openly and accurately about personal emotions, strengths and weaknesses. The truthfulness of how one can approach his/her limitations and articulate the areas that still need growth is a component of the confident and aware *self* which is not afraid of being vulnerable and transparent. The *self*'s desire to receive constructive feedback and not shy away from expressing a *self*-deprecating sense of humour is also considered a trait of confidence in the aware *self*. Therefore, part of the transformation of the *self* towards enabling authentic leadership requires a combination of *self*-discovery, *self*-disclosure/exposure related to the confidence aspect of an aware *self* and feedback solicitation in order to uncover unknown/blind areas of the *self* that one is not aware of but can be observable by others. "The issue of awareness of the *self* is made explicit in the theory of identity development proposed by Kegan (1982). In Kegan's model, growth of identity involves the person's ability to see the *self* with some objectivity, take different perspectives of one's *self* and observe it as from a distance. This is in contrast to the less developed state, where the *self* is more embedded (i.e., the subject), where the person is the *self* and is not able to observe and reflect on it" (Klenke, 2007). As such, *self*-awareness is not a destination point but an emerging process and continually evolving unravelling of the *self*.

5.3.2 *Self*- regulation

Another component of *self*-transformation for authentic leadership looks at the element of regulation of the *self*. According to Goleman's theorizing of emotional intelligence, signs of *self*-regulation include and are not limited to:

- Possessing or cultivating the propensity for reflection and thoughtfulness where rumination before reaction is viewed as key to regulating the *self*. Such a disposition is viewed as liberating one from being a prisoner to own feelings and emotions;
- Developing comfort with ambiguity and change in that continually transforming situations and environments do not evoke distress in the *self* and rather are viewed as inspiration and opportunity for creativity to emerge. The inspiration for creativity emerges by way of channelling one's rising feelings towards constructive input rather than reactivity.
- Fostering an ability to practice restraint and say 'no' to impulsive urges which if uncontrolled can contribute towards the decay of one's integrity. Such a practiced restraint is viewed as enabling an environment of trust and fairness in which people thrive rather than become demoralized by impulse driven outbursts. A demonstration of such integrity is key to authentic leader's influence for a wider follower base.

Avolio and Gardner posit that *self*-regulation "involves the processes whereby people exert *self*-control by (a) setting internal (either existing or newly formulated) standards, (b) assessing discrepancies between these standards and actual or expected outcomes, and (c) identifying intended actions for reconciling these discrepancies (Stajkovic & Luthans, 1998). Hence, *self*-regulation is the process through which authentic leaders align their values with their intentions and actions" (Avolio & Gardner, 2005).

5.3.3 Empathy

An authentic leader is considered an empathetic leader. Empathy displayed not in the form of appearing to please everyone but more towards the thoughtful consideration of feelings and other factors of those that surround a leader, i.e. employees. Although a display of such compassionate considerations is not deemed professional in most professional settings, empathy nevertheless facilitates heightened collaborations (Goleman, 2004). Goleman states that "empathy is particularly important today as a component of leadership for at least three reasons: the increasing use of teams; the rapid pace of globalization; and the growing need to retain talent."

In addition to the emotional intelligence connection of empathy, many leadership theories including authentic leadership emphasize that effective leader's exhibit a strong sense of empathy beyond the expression of mere sympathy. Therefore, part of the *self*-transformation towards authentic leadership entails developing a heightened sense for exercising empathy in everyday encounters and interactions. Although the research on empathy indicates that it is an innate trait in some, many experts indicate that given enough time and support, leaders can develop and enhance their empathy skills (Gentry, Weber, & Sadri).

5.3.4 Courage

Transforming the *self* into a courageous *self* is another important feature of developing authentic leadership skills. As in Kegan's model of the evolving *self* we understand third order adults to be in the conforming stage of their lives, while the fifth order and that which is linked with authentic leadership in this work, necessitates cultivating a courageous approach to how one leads and lives. Adopting a courageous approach to everyday interactions means the *self* is not threatened anymore by going against the crowd or becoming the black sheep when faced with opposition to what he/she believes in. Doing what the *self* believes to be right in the face of challenge and opposition takes a lot of inner strength. Authentic leadership entails "taking the road less travelled and doing, not what is easy, but what is right" (Sharma). The courageous *self* therefore has evolved in the awareness of *self* distinct from its surrounding such that it is no more influenced by an impending reaction and judgement by others but by an investment in preserving integrity and acting on the truth that *self*-belief holds.

5.4 How the *self* transforms

Referring back to Kegan's model of the evolving *self* explained earlier, this work suggests that there are certain factors that can influence the move for adults from the third order of the interpersonal balance to the fifth order of the interindividual balance. I posit that such a transformation or evolution of *self* can be realized through a combination of the factors to be discussed in the following paragraphs, or simply by virtue of one of the factors. I also make the claim that transformative spaces exist which are conducive to inspiring the *self* to transform. The case of transformative spaces will be dealt with in the next chapter as part of the case study.

In the Institutional balance of Kegan's model, he asserts that the strength of this stage is the identification and ownership of autonomy. He further elaborates that this very strength is also the institutional balance's weakness as the *self* becomes highly intertwined and embedded in this sense of autonomy. Which means this association with being an "autonomous" entity becomes an identity so much so that the weight of conforming to one's own fabricated standards may far outweigh the goal of truly being autonomous.

In Kegan's description of the evolution or transformation from the institutional balance to the fifth order of the interindividual balance, feelings of negative *self*-evaluation, feelings that one's personal institution or autonomy is threatened, and the fear of losing one's control and precious sense of being distinct, are put forth as the feelings that constitute the experience of losing the institutional balance and transforming into the next stage. As mentioned previously, loss is also viewed here as a source of transformation – be it a material or personal loss. In Kegan's theorizing, the loss is related to that of a former *self* which is put to death. The brewing discontent underlying the feelings mentioned above becomes the sign through which evolution is seen as taking shape and underway.

For the purposes of this work the conception of *self*-transformation is linked closely with the notion of *self*-actualization in Maslow's hierarchy of needs as explained earlier, the fifth order or the interindividual balance in Kegan's model of the evolving *self* is viewed in relationship to the attainment of Maslow's *self*-actualization stage of development. In the shift to the firth order, the sense of having left the moral world entirely and the killing of standards is what governs the newly evolved *self* where words such as "ought", "should", "must" are systematically removed from the vocabulary of the newly authentic *self*.

In addition to the element of a discontented *self* that is ripe for transformation, I posit that the factors below contribute towards either jumpstarting or accelerating an individual's transformation of the *self*.

5.4.1 Visiting and releasing the shadow

Renowned Swiss psychiatrist Carl Jung introduced the concept of the shadow to explain the second *self* in each one of us that remains mostly hidden and unexplored. The shadow is the most flawed and weakest part of us that we hide from others and that causes personal suffering laying in the depth of unconsciousness. The shadow in its make-up is a *self*-sabotaging agent that remains a road block to transformation if not confronted and investigated. Parts of us that we have disowned and repressed in fear of how others will perceive us make up the shadow. Trapped in societal notions of "good" vs "bad" resisting and suppressing the shadow consumes more energy and stifles experiencing the true and authentic *self*. In its repressed and denied state, the shadow according to Jung is projected onto others and externalized as another person's deficiencies.

If the shadow is such a dark place, then why would one need to visit it? According to Peggy Dulany, "the amount of energy it takes to hold down a repressed side of one's *self* is otherwise not available to living life (Dulany, 2012)." She continues:

> For anyone who wants to live consciously with their full creativity and energy, and to dedicate that to creating a better environment around us for our family and community or to honouring our commitments in the world, there is still another reason for tackling this difficult road into Shadowland. Armand Bytton, another wonderful teacher, states it so clearly: the same light and dark that is in ourselves is out there in the world. Only by recognizing and owning the dark that is in us will we be able to see and confront it out there. There are elements in our shadow selves that resonate with and may even help to replicate the darkness in the world if we do not explore, air and ultimately integrate those long-ago personal distortions into our larger *self*. If they fester and grow in the dark (our unconscious mind), they are likely to multiply and align themselves with aspects of the outside world that the rest of our *self* condemns or tries to change: a meanness, an exclusion, a *self*ishness, greed or destructive rage.

In *self*-transforming towards an authentic leader, the importance of visiting, releasing and then integrating our shadow *self* becomes ever more necessary in gaining consciousness over those aspects.

5.4.2 Exploring the "other"

Encounters with different types of people have the potential to engage individuals in an inner conversation of *self*-evaluation against the standards perceived in the external environment. I strongly believe that increasing such encounters and interactions with individuals outside of comfort zones can trigger queries within the *self*. As social creatures, and as ones mostly found within the third order in which Kegan explains is characterized by relating to "others", such frequented interactions with "others" who come from different experiences can have the potential to trigger transformation. Social learning theory it*self* posits that humans learn through interaction with and through others. In this realm, although the transformation process is to extract the *self* from the subject orientation and relation to others towards an object orientation of interpenetrability of *self* systems, the starting point for such a transformation can be ignited through querying interactions.

5.4.3 Expanding comfort zones

Risk taking is considered as one of the key behaviours leading towards *self*-actualization. It is the process through which the *self* encounters its boundaries and the extent to which it can push it*self*. Trying new things instead of sticking to safe paths creates a world of possibilities in which the *self* can experience many triggers for awakening and transformation. As Nicole Ann Ditz affirms, "*self*-actualization requires a great deal of risk taking, letting go of habitual and restrictive (though often comfortable) belief systems, stepping into the unknown, bringing one's attention back over and over again to observing compassionately one's inner experience, and dedicating one*self* day by day to the often strenuous process of change" (Ditz).

The next chapter will primarily deal with the case study of AWiB and will further explore the two factors of 'people' and 'risks' that constitute elements of *self*-transformation within the context of how transformative spaces enable such change and enable authentic female leadership.

CHAPTER SIX

When we quit thinking primarily about ourselves and our own self-preservation, we undergo a truly heroic transformation of consciousness.
~ Joseph Campbell

6. TRANSFORMATIVE SPACES – THE CASE OF AWIB

6.1 WHAT IS AWIB?

AWiB is a volunteer driven membership association that seeks to unleash potential through supporting the personal and professional development of career women and women in business in Ethiopia. It has been actively engaged in enabling such development by:

- facilitating experience sharing between upcoming and established female leaders through our networking platform;
- encouraging transformative conversations and sharing of pertinent information for personal and professional development through our monthly programs and annual events;
- convening prominent speakers and eminent personalities in an exchange of information and insights towards cultivating a culture of innovation, creativity and ideas exchange.
- providing a dynamic networking platform with networking exercises custom tailored to each monthly event.

AWiB offers women from diverse backgrounds and with diverse dreams, to come together and explore each other's paths – the challenges, the triumphs, the perseverance, the learning and ultimately the growth each one experiences in the multitude of encounters that surround one's personal and professional lives.

AWiB believes in the importance of leadership and entrepreneurship development for its members and beyond. When further exploring the above, we can define leadership as 'a way of thinking, listening, speaking and acting in a way that mobilizes the *self* and others into effective action, for the creation of a new possible future,' as Joseph Friedman defines it.

The AWiB *self* transformation stage takes shape once a month where a growing number of women convene, taking times out of their "busy" schedules to make time for themselves as they understand that one can never be too busy to grow. The notion of growth and development is the bedrock of what AWiB is about (Woldeyes). The increasing number of women at the monthly events demonstrated that AWiB was filling a key gap as it related to addressing issues of personal and professional development. Hence, in its 2012 restructuring, AWiB gave birth to a 15-person strong leadership team that resolutely works out of their own volition and volunteerism to support and enhance the growth journey of AWiB members and fans. As a platform for entry level and mid-level career women and female business owners, to date AWiB has brought prominent personalities, corporate CEOs, representatives from government agencies and international organizations, trainers, coaches to address current issues, raise awareness on pertinent personal and professional development topics.

One of AWiB's core attributes is in the provision of a networking platform for its members and fans. Not only does AWiB bring established leaders to engage with the audience in a highly accessible environment, but AWiB is also committed to profiling and introducing to its audience up and coming women and women whose work and contribution to society in their respective industries has not been exposed. AWiB believes in the power of creating and expanding networks for success, moving culturally imposed notions of reservation out of the equation. By promoting the value in building relationships, AWiB espouses the idea that a vision shared is a vision realized.

During networking sessions audience members are encouraged to leave their safety zones and engage in conversation with other women they have not discovered yet. These networking sessions, taking between thirty to forty-five minutes, are designed to foster conversation and ideas exchange on different topical issues, including leadership concepts.

In an effort to enable the skills development of its members, AWiB is highly relevant in its provision of an e-learning or electronically supported learning platform. To date, it has successfully launched two personal development 12-week courses led by an internationally certified life coach. Building on these efforts, AWiB aspires to bring more offerings to the repertoire of e-Education for personal and professional growth and further to this approach, some of the monthly meetings and annual forum sessions are premised upon skills transfer by bringing in established trainers and facilitators to engage participants in conversation and exchanges.

At the helm of AWiB's aspiration for its members is that a networking for excellence culture can take shape and emerge. Shared spaces and shared lessons can strengthen the pool of women in leadership positions by not only teaching but living the notion of sponsorship in addition to mentorship – where women pull each other to where their dreams take them. In all its endeavours AWiB strives to instil a "can do" attitude amongst its members, and provides them with the platform where knowledge, skills and attitudes to transform the "can do" into "done" can emerge.

As a membership association, all of AWiB's activities are supported through annual membership fees levied. Additionally, as of 2013 the association has been partnering with willing companies to sustain its activities.

Since the AWiB restructuring in early 2012, I have been engaged as part of the core leadership team in designing programs and providing strategic roadmap for the association. And in January 2013, I assumed the presidency of the association for a one-year term duration.

6.2 How does AWiB enable authentic leadership

As indicated in Chapter 3, the leading definition of authentic leadership which governs the analysis in this work is that of William L. Gardner and his two pronged approach. This is: i. *self*-awareness characterised by an in-depth understanding of personal emotions, identity and values; and ii. *Self-regulation* characterised by balanced processing of information and relational transparency of high levels of openness, *self*-disclosure and trust in close relationships, as intimated in Chapter 3. Furthermore, in discussing how AWiB enables authentic leadership amongst its members and frequenters, Avolio, Luthans and Walumba's definition indicates a very solid personal conviction and belief system as one of the defining characteristics of authentic leadership.

With the above points as guiding explanations to the approach of how AWiB enables authentic leadership, in the following section, I'll briefly draw parallels between the above definitions of authentic leadership and how they are embodied in AWiB's activities.

6.2.1 Networking

One of the primary reasons for which AWiB was formed was to challenge the norm for which women in Ethiopia come together. Given the Ethiopian social fabric and the numerous cultural obligations and responsibilities that women hold in continually weaving the social fabric, the balance between catering to *self* and others is tipped in favour of the latter. As caretakers within their society, Ethiopian women are the ones who carry the weight of executing commitments related to extended family, in addition to their own family and work obligations. The idea of taking time out for *self* advancement and promotion is a very novel concept in a society weighed by *yilugnta.*[3] Many women that frequent AWiB gatherings express how the need to conform to demands placed outside puts them in a position of responding to those demands firstly before catering to their own needs. In this case, AWiB caters to their need to be part of such support structures that enable their personal and professional development.[4]

Given the first response norm to cater to familiar circles, at each monthly event AWiB designs its sessions in such a way that for the first thirty to forty-five minutes of sessions, participants are put into groups to network through exercises designed to encourage interaction with women they have not met before. The objectives of the networking exercises are to enable women to: i. share personal impressions and stories; ii. build confidence in sharing the true *self* outside the confines of comfort; iii. build friendships and support systems through trust with other women who come to AWiB seeking similar endeavours.

6.2.2 Personal and professional development workshops

AWiB's personal and professional development workshops are administered through two different mediums. The first is through the monthly sessions convened which are a balance between informative topical issues and person development centred topics. These person development centred topics utilize the expertise and experience of resource persons who design the sessions in such a way as to elicit conversation among all attendants. They take on one specific element of authentic leadership and demonstrate through examples and exercises how ideals can be transformed into actionable outcomes and utilized in every day contexts.

---

3 Yilugnta is an Amharic word which is used to denote a state of waiving one's own immediate needs in favor of that of others so as to preserve harmony and save face. An individual exhibiting Yilugnta is one who is always predisposed to 'yes' even in times when his/her interests conflict to that of the request put forth. A characteristic marveled at in traditional circles, yilugnta has become the focus of many people's anxiety in modern days where the demands and pace of life in urban cities are stretching individuals beyond their capacity. Given women's multiple responsibilities in their family, social and work lives, the negative effects of yilugnta are exhibited much more in women who are faced with conundrum of performing against their true selves.

4 These impressions are acquired in oral sessions during the monthly programs.

Similarly, AWiB also holds *self*-confidence workshops for small groups. The workshop is led by an experienced resource person that has provided such workshops in different settings. The objective behind the *self*-confidence workshop is to encourage participants to look at themselves in a different light and explore the *self* and what it is made of in a celebration of the true *self*. The concept of looking behind the mask that we put up in our daily interactions is demonstrated through the use of real masks that participants put on and off as testimony to unearthing what is behind the *self* constructed mask.

As *self*-esteem and *self*-efficacy are the two key components of building confidence in *self*, the idea behind the monthly workshops is to support participants in looking at aspects of their lives in which they need to further invest and work towards unleashing their hidden unique traits and gifts from which they can derive the confidence to do, in addition to being. Part of this entails a closer examination of cultural attributes to which some of us fall prey, especially as it relates to speaking about ourselves and the contributions we are able to make in any setting.

The guiding principle behind the personal and professional development workshops is how building a sense of ownership through skills transfer is a building block towards *self* transformation. Recalling Chapter 3 and the various definitions of authentic leadership explored, the AWiB workshops reiterate that evolving change requires leaders with a stable philosophy of the *self*, as well as of others in the organization and community. And it is through such platforms that encourage reflection that these principles are put to the test and for the taking.

6.2.3 Experience sharing

"In the end, a person's authenticity is about more than just leadership. It's a reflection of one's inner spirit. When you're at peace with your*self*, you have more to offer the world and can freely share your own perceptions, ideas and beliefs" (Wagner). This statement by Tom Wagner is reflective of the element of experience sharing that AWiB aims to bring to its members and monthly attendees. During the monthly sessions, members are asked to share with the audience their personal experience of *self* transformation achieved through an element of inspiration either by attending sessions, workshops or simply through the exercise of sharing their own stories with others.

Additionally, experience sharing is also made possible through profiling and sharing the stories of women who have blazed trails and can serve as role models for other women on similar tracks. The visibility of such women is administered through annual events in which their stories are relayed by themselves and subject to a dialogue, as well as through harvesting these stories of personal challenges and triumphs for dissemination through print and web mediums. A lot of the feedback garnered from AWiB members emphasizes the importance of learning directly from the stories and personal experiences of other women.[5]

6.2.4 Web activities

AWiB's online presence makes up for the gap that comes in between monthly activities. The *self* transformative process for members and interested people does not end with face-to-face interactions but extends to the virtual realm. A section which is dedicated to articles on *self*-development harvests pertinent and diverse information ranging from managing stress to handling workplace conflict – all elements of effective leadership and hallmarks of authentic leadership as well. Additionally, a diverse number of Ethiopian women blog for AWiB on localized and observable issues as well as on topics that are within the realm of their expertise and knowledge. This aspect of AWiB's outreach is quite popular with readers who want to hear from other Ethiopian women on issues that matter to their female identity as well as the demands of culture, work and life in general. The commentary received in response to blog posts is also testament to how such sharing in a localized context facilitates reflection on the *self* in relations to the message conveyed by the authors who belong to the same social fabric as the readers.

6.3 What is the *Self*-transformation recipe of AWiB?

First and foremost, the AWiB principle of *self*-transformation for authentic leadership is premised on the recognition and acknowledgement that we all wear masks as we interact with the multitude around us. Such an

5 In the month of January 2013, I conducted up to 13 phone calls to registered members to inquire what aspect of AWiB was serving them and what was not. Although the phone calls I participated in making are thirteen, calls by other board members were made to our then membership base of around 150 women. It is from synthetisizing the feedback of these phone interviews conducted that I have arrived at the analysis that personal reflections on how to manage work and life balance are crucial to women in career.

acknowledgement reconciles the need to examine and remove our masks to lead from an authentic place. The AWiB model of authentic leadership is highly linked with a personal journey strongly tied to relinquishing the obsession of what others think of us and how they perceive us. This more than normal preoccupation of what others think of us is considered to disguise or manipulate aspects of our personality that we fear will be subject to judgement if personality is not in alignment with expectations of others. Conforming to expectations rather than responding to *self* values and beliefs is considered under the AWiB transformative space as seeking approval rather than an expression of an authentic *self*.

Secondly, the AWiB approach to *self*-transformation is premised upon openness towards taking risks and challenging fear. In a position of exercising leadership, taking a risk could mean not being afraid of making a mistake and doing what needs to be done or said without the fear of failure. Likewise and intertwined with removing the masks we were, taking the risk to speak and behave in accordance with one's personal and most important values in the face of possible rejection is an act of authentic leadership that AWiB aspires to instil in members and participants understanding of *self*-transformation through the many channels it utilizes to influence.

Thirdly, cultivating a sense of ownership and responsibility is an element promoted in the ideals of what AWiB aims to achieve in its recipe for *self*-transformation in our society. By taking responsibility for our experiences, thoughts and feelings, the concept of ownership defers the inclination to externalize sources of misfortunes or challenges that one may experience. Such a positioning and understanding that we affect the circumstances in our lives take away blame and excuses as the hallmarks of an unsuccessful life and can inspire the will to change the situation that one finds him*self*/her*self* immersed in.

Fourthly, AWiB espouses a predisposition to continuous learning and discovery processes within the *self*. The enabling environment that AWiB provides is supported by both human and information resources that are made available for members and participants to further explore their individual potential. Creating an environment conducive to unleashing potential through *self*-discovery and transformation is one of the leading ingredients in AWiB's leadership recipe. A core attribute of this ingredient is exemplified through vicarious experiences attained by coming into contact with other women with similar background and yet different trajectories in their life paths. The learning that happens through an open and transparent exchange is of paramount importance as part of the reflective journey towards *self*-transformation.

"There is a clear ethical and moral dimension in demonstrating and developing authentic leadership. Because authentic leaders are clear about their values, goals and motives, they understand the meaning of what they do and they lead for a higher purpose (Zielinska)." This element of envisioning for a higher purpose is the fifth and most important *self* transformation recipe of AWiB which in a way holds all the others. Challenging mediocrity and not accepting to settle for less in terms of what each individual's contribution is to their family, society, community and life in general – the outer purpose. And committing to awaken and *self*-transform – the inner purpose. Eckhart Tolle makes this delineation between an outer and inner purpose while still maintaining that one cannot be dealt with without addressing the other. He continues:

> *As soon as you rise above mere survival, the question of meaning and purpose becomes of paramount importance in your life. Many people feel caught up in the routines of daily living that seem to deprive their life of significance. Some believe life is passing them by or has passed them by already. Others feel severely restricted by the demands of their job and supporting a family or by their financial or living situation. Some are consumed by acute stress, others by acute boredom. Some are lost in frantic doing; others are lost in stagnation. Many people long for the freedom and expansion that prosperity promises. Others already enjoy the relative freedom that comes with prosperity and discover that even that is not enough to endow their lives with meaning. There is no substitute for finding true purpose. But the true or primary purpose of your life cannot be found on the outer level. It does not concern what you do but what you are – that is to say, your state of consciousness* (Tolle, 2005).

As demonstrated in the above explanations of what constitutes AWiB's approach to *self*-transformation, parallels can be drawn to the analysis provided in Chapter 5 where several factors were identified as comprising the evolution from the third order to the fourth and fifth orders in Kegan's model of the evolving *self*. The next section will look at concrete examples of session hosted by AWiB that have primarily focused on the transformational *self*.

6.3.1 Examples of work on *self*-transformation

In further exploring the role AWiB plays in enabling authentic female leadership through *self*-transformation, the following section gives a summary of some of the monthly sessions hosted and the intention with which the programs were developed.

6.3.1.1 Rediscovering our worth

A workshop delivered in March 2012, *Rediscovering our Worth* was a session facilitated by a leadership consultant and international facilitator with the primary objective of inviting participants to take personal time off and take part in an interactive and participatory process of rediscovering and connecting to *self*. The process entailed gaining and understanding of the *self* profile or what really energizes a person by responding to the following questions:

- What's your purpose? What's your passion?
- What kind of contribution do you wish to make to the world?
- What are the best qualities you express in your relationships?

The driving principle was that an understanding of *self* and connection to *self* empowers one to unlock potential towards living the life one desires. As part of the authentic leadership building aspect of the session, the personal dynamics that were addressed during the conversations included:

- Challenges experienced in picking things that one cared about (lack of clarity of *self*);
- Insecurity experienced in individual decision making strategies (lack of confidence);
- Putting more priority for other people's agenda over that *self* in an ultimate sacrifice of personal needs (conforming);
- Believing more in other people's conviction rather than personal beliefs (lack of assertiveness);
- Doing every day or often tasks not connected to one's purpose and what one believes in (in-authenticity).

In this exercise participants were confronted with the difference between the three different profiles we all have: i. the professional profile; ii. the social profile; and iii. the *self* profile wherein the questions related to defining one's essence, commitment, contribution and purpose were contained. As part of the inner most profile of the *self* the *self*-profile exercise opened up a platform for the female participants that had gathered that evening to confidently declare their intentions were a modest culture would usually not permit one to freely engage as such. Some responses that were recorded that evening in response to the question of what feelings best described a great moment in their lives:

- Empowered
- Complete

- Confident
- Belonging
- Curious
- Elated
- Mesmerized
- Liberated
- Blissful
- satisfied
- blessed
- thankful
- happy
- peaceful

In collectively drawing upon and strengthening the *self* profile, the exercise was resourceful in conveying to participants the critical part of the authentic leader – the "I am" – from where one can reach in and find sustenance and derive strength from during period of trials and tribulations. Ultimately, the *self*-aware individual as described in Chapter 5 is an authentic leader. Hence, this particular session on Rediscovering Our Worth, was a crucial part of AWiB's work as a transformative space enabling an environment for female participants to share tools and ideas on a reflective approach to *self*-awareness.

6.3.1.2 The Mysticism of Personal Power

In an April 2012 session, AWiB looked into the aspect of personal power as a component of building authentic leadership. Noting that there are several dimensions to how an individual can access power, the departure point and objective of this session was to refer individuals to the personal power derived not from positional placement but rather from the *self*. Baan, Long and Pearlman define personal power as the "ability to use energy and drive to manifest wise actions in the world for the greater good, while being aware of one's influences on a situation" (Baan, Long, & Pearlman). Not understanding this aspect of human ability is considered as one of the biggest problems by Lao Tzu – a famous Chinese philosopher – almost two thousand five hundred years ago. His premise was that individuals experienced themselves as powerless.

In this regard, AWiB identified the following focal points to drive the discussion during the session entitled the *Mysticism of Personal Power*:

- When people do not have a sense of power they become resentful and uncooperative;
- Individuals who do not feel personal power feel fear;
- Individuals who dominate others are, in fact, enslaved by their fear.

A further driving point during the session was to look at personal power as the ability to achieve what ones wants – in essence, as the building blocks for success and happiness. This point is especially relevant in preceding discussion of ownership and taking personal responsibility as one of the elements of realizing authentic leadership. In articulating individual definitions of what personal power is and means to them, some respondents reflections are captured as below:

- Fearlessness as power; "I am not afraid"
- Power is energy that we can gather;
- To be with my*self* and be able to travel the path I choose to travel is an embodiment of personal power
- How much I give and how much I give to others is an expression of personal power
- Power is what you get from others to make you feel strong
- Power is to influence others and have them do what we want them to do
- Power is being *self*-sufficient
- Power is being aware of one's capabilities
- Power is how I have satisfied and influenced others;
- Power is one's authority over *self* – others don't tell us what personal power is. We are always powerful regardless of our successes and failures;
- Power is truth and faith;

In summary, participants shared that trusting the divine, *self*-knowledge and their individual accomplishments comprised what personal power was for them. Whereas many expressed they felt powerful when they were helping people; when experiencing more in life; when contributing; when getting through a to-do list; when loving *self*; when giving; when challenged; when sharing knowledge with others; in situations that are in alignment with personal values and when standing for what they believe in. And on the contrary, many expressed that doubting, anger, irritation, blaming, not taking responsibility for own life defined for others moments when and how they give away their personal power. [6]

6.3.1.3 Non-violent Communication – The Practice of Life Serving Communication[7]

The NVC workshop AWiB hosted was held in September 2013 and facilitated by me. Ever since my return to Ethiopia I have become much more aware and conscious of language and the embedded and underlying messages that are flung in between basic words. Most importantly I realized how intricate the relationship between culture and language is, imbued with notions of guilt, judgment and sarcasm meant to fly off as humour, yet heavily laden with inauthentic expressions. The lack of compassion and authenticity I witnessed in employee and employer relationships at a basic level inspired to share what I know of the NVC process to collectively motivate ourselves to observe closely communication styles and monitor assumptions made around what is stated and what is actually heard. Underscoring the basic assumptions inherent in this method, as indicated below, the interactive workshop aimed to reposition how people perceived violent communication. The basic assumptions of the NVC process communicated to the group of attendees:

- A natural state of compassion that we all possess;
- At the root of misunderstandings and conflict are unmet needs;
- Unexpressed feelings alienate us from our source of empathy;
- We later pay for short term results gained through the use of guilt, shame, blame and obligation.

In the relationship between authentic leadership development and communication, introducing the concept of compassionate communication is crucial for the following reasons:

---

6 I captured these responses during the April 2012 session on the Mysticism of Personal Power.

7 Non-violent Communication or NVC is a communication method developed by Dr. Marshall B. Rosenberg and based on the priciples of non-violence. The method assumes that we all have a natural state of compassion that we all possess; at the root of mistunderstanding and conflict are unmet needs; unexpressed feelings alienate us from our source of empathy; and we later pay for short term results gained through the use of guilt, shame, blame and obligation.

- to improve morale, strengthen group dynamics and reduce work conflict;
- to improve productivity, creativity & work performance;
- to support getting out of role and back into being humans.

One of the key attributes of an authentic leader is his/her ability to listen. In the NVC process developed by Dr. Marshall B. Rosenberg, active listening is a key component of communicating compassionately. Through active listening and other components of the NVC process, authentic leaders are capacitated with the ability to foster authentic conversations within their respective organizations. Mazutis and Slawinski propose that "strategic leaders who exhibit authentic leadership capabilities (*self*-awareness, relational transparency, unbiased processing, and *self*-regulation) will tend to create a culture in which authentic conversations are encouraged" (Mazutis & Slawinksi). They continue, "Authentic conversations support the feed-forward flow of learning specifically by allowing for unbiased, open and transparent communications between the individual and group levels and then the group and organizational level through the process of intuiting, interpreting, integrating and institutionalizing" (Mazutis & Slawinksi).

In the NVC process, *unbiased* communication feeds directly to the first component of observing without evaluating, which is critical to authentic leaders' assessment of any situation – especially at the organizational level where leaders at various levels can step in as conflict transformation agents simply by how they receive, interpret and convey information.

During the workshop, I explained some concepts related to conflict transformation, perception & conflict, life-alienating communication, developing a feelings list to convey different feelings and emotions that surface in different encounters. Additionally, the element of how to express feedback in a non-violent way was discussed. A majority of the session was directed towards participants framing a personal disagreement or conflict they have encountered through the four part NVC process of observations, feelings behind observations, needs related to the feelings experienced and concrete requests to be made in direct correlation to transforming the disagreement or conflict.

The feedback derived from participants who attended the workshop was positive in the sense that many acknowledged the need to communicate compassionately and how now they had developed the lens to view conversations as purpose driven rather than habitual exchanges.

6.3.1.4 Appreciative inquiry

Nurturing a culture of appreciation is an objective within AWiB's female leadership development model. This approach is of high significance in AWiB's activities based on an identification that the most common or normative way of creating efficiency and maximizing productivity at both a personal and organizational level is to approach it from a problem-solving orientation. While heeding the benefits of the problem oriented approach, AWiB finds value in the Appreciative Inquiry (AI) approach to enabling change within organizations and environments as well as at the individual level. Harnessing this value of appreciation, AWiB's October session hosted an AI practitioner and trainer to work with participants in looking at their approach to transforming *self,* systems and organizations through the AI lens.

The workshop was a call inviting participants to focus on possibilities instead of problems. According to the trainers, AI is an exploration of what gives life to human systems when they function at their best. It is based on the assumption that individuals, teams, and institutions all move in the direction of the questions they ask and encourages questions about what we want more of in ourselves, in our relationships and in our communities. Based on positive questions leading to the discovery of what works well so we can do more of it, rather than inquiring into what did not work as well to do less of it.

According to the trainer Bezawit Bekele, in the AI process "a clear, concise topic is chosen, positive questions are developed. Stories start to develop; patterns begin to emerge. Individuals recall and tap into positive achievements and stories that strengthen and inspire" (Bekele, 2012). This is not only true of transforming systems and organizations, but also quite useful in assessing personal attributes and strengths towards accelerating *self*-transformation by looking at the *self* in a kind and gentle way. The *self*-awareness requirement inherent to authentic leadership can be further capitalized on by utilizing an Appreciative Inquiry approach to the *self.*

Leadership Development consultant, Nadia Waber, who is also a practitioner of AI and board member of AWiB refers to the meaning of the two words to better understand the basis of Appreciative Inquiry:

- *Appreciation* means to recognize and value the contributions or attributes of things and people around us.
- *Inquiry* means to explore and discover, in the spirit of seeking to better understand, and being open to new possibilities.

"So, what this means is that by appreciating what is good and valuable in the present situation, we can discover and learn about ways to effect positive change for the future. It is also about a paradigm shift, looking at the glass as half empty or half full and the effects of our understanding in every situation" (Waber).

Waber continues:

> As we accomplish a mission through great leaders, the concept of AI focuses on leadership by which we all have the potential to become one and therefore relate to all. What must leaders look for in those they lead? Leadership is a process by which members of a group are empowered to work towards a shared goal or a shared vision that will create change, hence a call for appreciative leadership. A leader must seek what each person has in him or in her that enables transformation. It is also about looking into one's own paradigm as well as looking into others paradigm and appreciating what's in all of us. Leadership is about affirming what each person brings to the table, to this shared goal. The Appreciative Inquiry model is based on the assumption that the questions we ask will tend to focus our attention in a particular direction. Some other methods of assessing and evaluating a situation and then proposing solutions are based on a *deficiency* model. "What are the problems?", "What's wrong?" or "What needs to be fixed?" "When we change the way we look at things, the things will look at change". What we focus more gets bigger (Waber).

Similarly, in an application of the above thoughts on *self*-transformation, the AI approach entails introspection and an evaluation of what an individual has done so well that he/she would like to do more of. By focusing on these positive attributes, further potential can be built up in derived from the confidence to look at *self* in such a positive light.

6.3.1.5 Tapping into You Potential - AWiB listens

This is another monthly session that was designed for women only using the World Café methodology of conversation. The methodology created by Juanita Brown and David Isaacs in the late 1990s, aims to foster collaborative dialogue, sharing mutual knowledge, and discovering new opportunities for action. The objective for that session as set by AWiB was for authentic reflections to be made in a safe and transparent environment in which the potential for seedlings of *self*-transformation to take root in everyone can be supported.

The set up for the World Cafe' entailed distributing participants into roundtables and posing one question which they were asked to deliberate upon collectively for twenty minutes. At the end of the twenty minutes, they would be asked to again disperse into different tables, initiating them to meet and exchange ideas with other women they had not met yet or conversed with.

The central questions posed for the evening were:

- Without being shy, as a woman, what unique qualities do I express?
- What elements of our culture may be holding us back from fulfilling our full potential?
- Where will I be when we overcome our challenges? Together, where will we be?

The questions were designed to be reflective and encourage introspection. Additionally, in its design, the questions were also geared to promote an appreciative inquiry method of addressing issues that arise. Rather than lamenting on the deficits of culture and how it negatively impacts potential fulfilment, the way out of that analysis was to guide participants into looking at elements of personal responsibility, personal power and ownership is driving their dreams and *self* transformative processes in direction they desired.

In essence, here are highlights of the responses collected for each question:

Without being shy, as a woman, what unique qualities do I express?
The answers collected from each table indicate that women were recognizing other women as having limitless femininity and power; having the capacity to love deeply, to hold and balance different roles in the various spectrums of their existence in society. Resilience, patience, fearlessness, spontaneity, perseverance, care, adaptability, flexibility and authenticity were some qualities expressed in response.

What elements of our culture may be holding us back from fulfilling our full potential?
In response to the above question, the following answers emerged during the reflection session:

- Norms in one's culture
- Society's enforcement of Do's and Don'ts
- Living in a patriarchal and hierarchical culture
- Lack of female role models (or lack of knowledge of those that exist)
- Pre-defined roles/ expectations for women and men
- Expectation for women to be shy
- Personal mind-set

- Experience of double-burden (multiple roles)
- Women's own sense of guilt

Out of these responses, questions also emerged from within the groups:

- How do we, as women create our own culture?
- How are we perpetuating certain practices in our culture? Does this serve us?
- How are we creating systems that are confining us?
- If we wish to see change, do we live what we speak?

Where will I be when we overcome our challenges? Together, where will we be?

Participants responded that they looked forward to creating a community for themselves and others in which:

- there is more freedom and creativity, and one can be more authentic;
- women's calibre is expressed in every arena of life, and where they become bolder
- there is a shift in attitude
- women are not making sacrifices anymore
- there is equal pay
- perceptions on motherhood as a 'deficit' shift to a positive one;
- there is harmony in the family, and thus, in society
- women feel liberated in the most private areas of their lives
- one writes one's own life script
- witness global peace with women in leadership
- share more experiences of who we are as women
- explore many career and passion options
- the world can tap more into women's potential

This particular session was important as a building block for authentic leadership in the sense that it provided participants the tools to *self* reflect in together with others, feeding off on the energy and knowledge that others provided. Many explained that they left the session highly energized and exhilarated about the possibilities that lay ahead of them.

6.3.1.6 Genuine Contact Workshop

This workshop was designed specifically for members under the leading theme *getting in genuine contact with your life's purpose* and led by an international coach and certified Genuine Contact trainer. Designed for personal development and with a specific focus on individual health balance, the workshop was intended to assist participants in identifying areas of overextension and neglect in our respective lives. By providing simple tools and *self*-reflection exercises, the workshop encouraged participants to re-connect with their life's purpose by identifying the obstacles holding one back from moving a vision forward.

> Within the Genuine Contact program, the Medicine Wheel Tool serves as the overall matrix to guide learning, healing, development, evolution and consciousness that brings about results that exceed expectations. The Medicine Wheel Tool assists action/reflection learning regarding health and balance in the organization focusing on purpose, leadership, vision, community, management and relationships. Workshop participants are taught to use this framework as a tool for achieving and then maintaining health and balance (Turk).

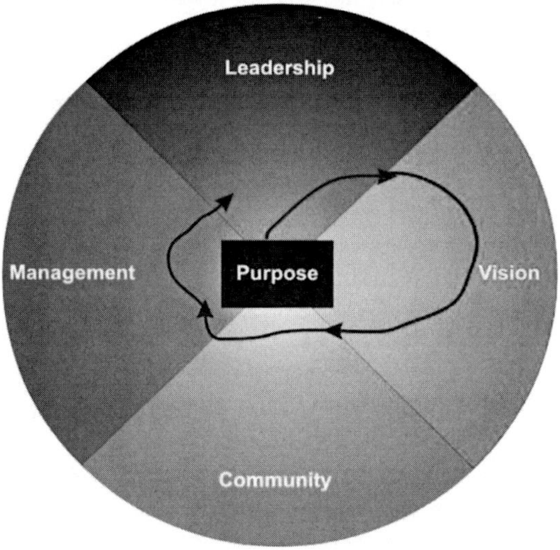

According to this approach, an individual finds purpose at the intersection of the four quadrants that constitute the medicine wheel. By initiating *self* query at the leadership quadrant and proceeding clock-wise, a number of questions are posed at each quadrant to enable arrival at a deeper understanding of that component. In the leadership quadrant for example, our capacity to achieve our purpose is examined. What we do as leaders, how we do it and most importantly the status of inner *self* and our will to achieve our purpose is queried to develop a deeper answer. The leading question then becomes, where am I doing well, living my purpose and where can I strengthen?

In the vision quadrant, we articulate the future that we want to emerge and the questions leading the reflection are:

- What do I see when I achieve my purpose?
- What do I hear?
- What do I say?
- What do I feel?
- What do I know?

In the community quadrant, the internal and external stakeholders, the environment we create for achieving our purpose and vision are identified. By recognizing who the key people we spend our time with are, we assess in this quadrant whether or not they hinder us from achieving our life's purpose. Lastly, the management quadrant is about ensuring the systems, structures and supports are in place and help us to identify and remove barriers to achieving our goals (Turk).

In concluding this section, it is worthy to reiterate the transformative nature of the space that AWiB has created, by contextualizing it within Jack Mezirow's Transformative Learning Theory. In essence, the various sessions and opportunities for growth that AWiB cultivates are part of diversifying and offering mediums of learning towards *self*-transformation. According to Mezirow, there are four processes of learning.

The first is to elaborate an existing point of view by seeking more evidence to support the initial assumption. Secondly, we learn by establishing new points of view through encountering a new group. Thirdly, learning can be accomplished by transforming our point of view through experiences or encounters that result in our critically reflecting on our thought processes. A repetition of this process according to Mezirow can lead to "transformation by accretion in our governing habit of mind" (Mezirow). Lastly, he postulates that we may transform our habit of mind by becoming aware and critically reflective, noting that such transformations are rare as long as what we learn fits comfortable in existing frames of reference.

Therefore, the learning and transformation occurs when confronted with that which stretches one beyond his/her comfort zone. In this regard, AWiB is introducing concepts, ideas, exercises and encounters that trigger an introspective exercise amongst the women that frequent the sessions and learning opportunities provided, thereby being the conducive transformative space in which *self*-transformation occurs for authentic leadership.

In the following chapter, experiences of *self*-transformation through the AWiB platform will be shared from accumulated testimonies and my own personal reflection.

CHAPTER SEVEN

If you want to awaken all of humanity, then awaken all of yourself. If you want to eliminate the suffering in the world, then eliminate all that is dark and negative in yourself. Truly, the greatest gift you have to give is that of your own self-transformation. ~ Lao-Tzu

7. EXPERIENCES OF *SELF* TRANSFORMATION

7.1 FEEDBACK ON IMPACT OF AWIB ON *SELF*-TRANSFORMATION

This chapter is dedicated to responding to the third question raised in Chapter 2 on how organized platforms enable *self*-transformation and authentic leadership among urban Ethiopian women. The following all constitute an answer towards one of the three research questions put forth in this work.

- Testimonies provided by women who frequent AWiB sessions
- Responses given by respondents to questions on AWiB's impact
- My personal experience of *self*-transformation.

7.1.1 Testimonies

The following are a few testimonies[8] provided by participants on their experiences of the various sessions and mediums that AWiB utilizes in enabling *self*-transformation.

> *The Women of Excellence award event was a beautiful event and was amazed to see so many dynamic and interesting people under one roof. I was touched by the stories of the nominees and what each one of them has achieved and more so by the challenges they had overcome. Appreciation is an energy that when given out comes back to reward you with more and more so I am sure that more centres of excellence and potential will be awoken because of this spirit of appreciation.*

~

> *I noticed the group of women that I spent my day with today have beautiful minds and they all shared their experiences in different ways which wouldn't be possible without this session. I was surprised to find out we all wear masks at different times or places but we don't know it. I am disappointed it took me*

[8] It is common practice for AWiB to collect feedback at the end of every session through feedback forms that participants are asked to fill.

longer time to discover and master the good personal skills/qualities that I have by avoiding to talk about myself and being modest.

~

I was surprised to find that good environment encourages explaining your feelings without fear. I plan to be part of AWiB. I really, really longed to be part of this day and so happy. It is more than what I expected. Thank you, AWiB.

~

First of all I would like to thank you for an amazing idea of this association. I have been in a managerial position for about 5 years now and I never had a chance to meet people or develop my knowledge/share ideas outside my business circle. AWiB gave me that and that's why I didn't even sleep on the idea of being a member and acted after my very first attendance.

~

From today's conference, I have seen the following: It's inspirational, gives networking opportunity, and helps our professional and personal growth.

~

I learned that I have everything inside me to unleash and become confident.

~

I was surprised to find that it is possible not to wear an invisible mask at all. I learned that values such as trust and kindness are related to self-confidence. I plan to get rid of my mask and build up my self-confidence for the better. I was surprised to find out that justification is a sign of lacking self-confidence. We shouldn't worry about what other people think about us. We need to trust, see ourselves and do what we believe is right.

~

I discovered that confidence starts with trust. I also learned that wearing masks can harm self-confidence. Because it's about hiding your true self; not showing your identity to other people is also not showing it to yourself. I noticed that confidence is about small things we do every day. What strikes people are details.

~

I was surprised in the self-assessment my confidence level got to excellent as opposed to what I thought it to be. I plan to continuously develop my self-confidence with AWiB team I met today.

~

I relearned that developing confidence is highly important and it is the engine that moves everything.

7.1.2 Responses on *self*-transformation

The following question was posed to some AWiB frequenters to better understand the effect of the programs on their development and *self* transformation.

In what way has AWiB programming impacted your *self*-transformation process? How has it contributed to your leadership skills?

The respondents were chosen based on the number of sessions they have attended. Given that in my request for feedback, I have informed the respondents that their responses will be anonymous, their names will not be revealed in the responses below:

Respondent 1

From those sessions I was able to attend, reading some of the blogs and some of the stories on successful women, I found out that life is not easy; success doesn't come easy. Rather it requires determination and hard work. When we fix our eyes on our prize/goals be it as a professional woman, as a mom, a wife and other socially given responsibilities we would be successful. AWiB has helped me to see myself, to reflect deep down, to look for opportunities and to mingle with likeminded women. All the sessions I have attended made me to think about life and all it surrounded, proactively and cautiously. It also helps me not to access the status quo and rather to push the bar for myself and for others too.

Respondent 2

For me, AWiB has impacted myself transformative process by making me stop and think what my strengths are and what areas of improvement I have to work on. By sharing successful as well as not-so-successful experiences, I have started a journey of self-transformation. I have learned that leadership skills start with leading oneself. Leadership is not about never making a mistake, it's about owning responses to my own and others needs in such a way that we can collectively move together, to a better destination. My leadership skills have improved in terms of upping my emotional intelligence as well.

Respondent 3

"I see AWiB as the right beginning of "me" thinking! Like I always say I was this kind of woman who is very dedicated to my company and still I am, but I neglected one big portion of the world... that is "ME". Of course one grows through the work path but that is not the only one way which fills your soul. I

was even to the extent thinking like if I go out of work early I cannot be a good example/role model to my team... even feeling unfaithful to my company. The reason I did not even think of going for my second degree accounts for the same reason. But I proved myself wrong after I joined AWiB and started to look really deep inside me. I saw myself being transformed and learning a lot more than I imagined... I became a better role model EVER and even regretted I was a bit late to join this dynamic association. Honestly speaking whenever I come to AWiB I feel like I am going one step forward in my thinking and "way how" of being the "right me". Of course I became a little bit selfish too and that is healthy I guess... it's good to live for people but living for yourself is also equally important. So there are three MAJOR turning points in my life which in fact was hard to decide on but transformed me to the better: i. choosing my career path in 2004; ii. calling off my wedding in 2011 (too personal but necessary to mention); and iii. joining AWiB and Rotary Club in 2012. Trust me those decisions transformed me to be a more blooming flower and a more strong change agent to myself and others I lead.

Respondent 4

I feel being an AWiB Board member is contributing to my growth, positively impacting how I think and feel about my surroundings. I feel more resilient when responding to challenges, open to find creative solutions and confident that within the AWiB network I will find the resources and support I need. I feel more optimistic about the future and the potential that can be unleashed within individuals and organizations, in an innovative way.

On AWiB's impact on my leadership skills, it has made me more decisive, as I work with my team-mates and works towards the development of AWiB itself. I notice that I feel more comfortable to express myself fully, using 'tough love' when needed, and kindness at other instances, depending on what is required in the moment. I feel that through AWiB I have renewed my commitment to serve our community of members (and beyond), for the benefit of their own personal and professional lives. In my leadership, I feel I have moved into having a broader view of our work, beyond the confines of an individual organization, looking at a whole sector and system, and reflecting on how to impact that, through fostering collaboration."

Respondent 5

My involvement in AWIB has helped me grow tremendously as a leader. Thus far, it has taught me how to aim high and be bold; which are markings of a good leader.

Respondent 6

AWIB and the Women of Excellence program in particular has helped me learn the kind of qualities I want to foster in myself as a woman leader. I've also learnt from the impressive leadership of the Executive Committee, and I've benefitted from being accountable for my assigned tasks.

Respondent 7

It made me think about myself, and how I design my future in my terms. It helped me to know authentic people that model what I really want to see in myself. It pushes me to high standard of excellence and never be satisfied with my status quo. It makes me think of how to develop others and devise ways with others. It sets the bar higher and higher not leaving room for mediocrity. It brought women nearer who could be model of excellence for me to emulate their life styles. It opened my eyes for the need to grab opportunities for learning comes by doing, leading and being pro-active in life. It constantly reminds me that women have a long way to go so making the way is one of my role. It availed me a blogging forum where I can express my ideas and interact with others. I am work in progress, learning, growing up, leading and being transformed by doing. It surrounded me with able, confident, positive, knowledgeable and resourceful board members who force me to widen my horizon. In the midst of a struggling society, AWiB gave me believers of better future for women, thriving women who believe that change is inevitable for Ethiopian women and we are a living example to making those changes happen by doing our parts of the equation.

Respondent 8

AWiB programming impacted my self-transformation process in a visible way. Before I joined AWiB, I thought I was the only women or I was among very few bold women to speak out loud and influence others. Now, I know there are many other women playing the same role even more to change their lives and the life of others. I am encouraged to be myself than changing to the norm; which is being shy or timid like most of the professional as well as the non-professional women around me. This gives me strength and energy to keep going as a leader.

Respondent 9

Being an active member at AWiB is my attempt to demonstrate to women that this stifling cultural norms stated above can be reversed if we have a clear understanding of our purpose and if we believe in ourselves enough to realize our dream. I thank all board members for allowing me make at least some contribution to this cause.

I was happy to volunteer to join AWiB board because it gave me an opportunity to witness first hand that capable Ethiopian women leaders can transform society. It has inspired me to dream bigger and to believe that if I can set my mind and heart to it that not only can I aim for and reach higher heights but also lead others to do the same. My time with the AWiB board was much treasured and personally for me it was a tremendous learning and networking opportunity.

Respondent 10

AWiB has enabled me to clearly understand my worth and thus has enabled me to constantly practice living up to my worth. The monthly programme and trainings that are provided helped me rediscover myself and strengthened my commitment to myself (leadership).

7.1.3 Telephone interviews

As part of the AWiB leadership team's interest in collecting information on members' experience of their interaction with AWiB and its activities, board members were assigned the task of conducting phone surveys and interviews with members in January 2013. Of the eleven women I was assigned to interview, I wish to share the response of two who gave their time freely and expressed succinctly their experience of AWiB. A few of the other respondents were not reachable while at least three were inactive members who could not say much to the *self*-transformative aspect to AWiB programming.

Respondent 1

Respondent 1 works as an auditor in an international non-governmental organization (INGO). She has been attending the AWiB sessions consistently since signing up for membership in July 2012. She states that since signing on as a member, she has only missed one event. She particularly enjoys the experience sharing element of the sessions where she states that she draws inspiration from and has helped her look at her life and contributions in a different manner. Similarly, the respondent found the networking sessions quite beneficial and in fact formed a friendship with someone new through the networking session, enabling her to break out of the normative approach of forming friendships. The respondent also stated that she finds highly useful the lifestyle articles that are disseminated through the AWiB site and also took the opportunity to attend online the *self*-development workshop which she expresses having benefited from immensely.

Respondent 2

Respondent 2 is an entrepreneur with her own import/export business. As it relates to AWiB programming, she replied that she enjoys all the sessions delivered and the thematic focus of the monthly topics. She considers her*self* to be someone invested in her personal development and therefore why she is grateful for this platform. She explained that she has never been part of such a platform and the learning she derives from the AWiB effect has been transformational for her and an awakening experience. Similarly, the respondent has attended the *self*- confidence workshops provided by AWiB which she explains she found insightful.

7.1.4 My personal journey with AWiB

As indicated briefly in the author's perspective section, my personal journey with AWiB began three months after I had moved back to the country of my birth, Ethiopia. Throughout 2011 I managed to attend a few of the sessions just as a participant and I was quite enamoured by the topics of discussion as well as the personality of the co-founders which shone brightly. The ease with which they discussed personal and professional matters and the way they held the space resonated with me immensely.

By the end of 2011, I had been quite active with a number of women's groups and from related burnout had arrived at the conclusion that I did not fit my context. Resolute with the idea that I had changed too much over the years and therefore could not fit my environment, I had also reached the decision that perhaps it was time to move on to a new place where I felt that I could fit better. In dealing with the burn-out I had experienced, I took six weeks off and went abroad to take time to rejuvenate and replenish my*self*. It was about a few weeks later that I received an email from the founder and the then President, asking me to join a leadership team of fifteen women who would comprise the Board in the restructuring of AWiB. Given that my experience of AWiB had been a positive one, the request was not something I had to contemplate too much. I accepted and joined as of February 2012.

Over the span of four months since joining the leadership team, the amount of time I spent tending over AWiB activities and demands consumed much of my energy and time. The energy spent however did not deplete me as it was coming from a place of volunteerism that was creating abundant energy in me rather than depletion energy. By the time I reached my second year of service, many were amazed at the dedication and commitment I have given to an initiative which does not reward monetarily. Nevertheless, I have come to learn that the learning I derive from giving my time and energy to AWiB has been priceless.

In a culture that has not really taken up the concept of volunteerism, I felt motivated to devote my energy towards a cause I believe in and from which I derive a sense of *self*-fulfilment. While the perception may be that volunteerism is only about giving, the reality for me has been that I have come to expand my network, build my communication skills, enhance my confidence, learn different management techniques and learn to be an overall focused and committed person with a much more positive outlook on life, my*self* and my potential and possibilities. Referring back to the discussion of linking authentic leadership with Abraham Maslow's description of *self-actualization* as the realization and development of one's personal capacities, I feel the transformation I have experienced being part of AWiB has greatly impacted the progress I am making in attaining my need for *self-actualization.*

Additionally, my confidence level has soared and I witnessed my*self* transform from someone who was shy to address a small group of people to someone who found no qualms about getting up on stage, holding the space and addressing a room full of 500 plus people. I see this as testimony to building authentic leadership skills of which courage at its basic form is one of them.

Moreover, the learning and transformational experience has been quite immense in that the responsibilities I have assumed required me to *self*-reflect on a daily basis. Constantly checking in to ensure that decisions I make, actions that I take and behaviours I exhibit are in unceasing alignment with my core values. Because of the commitment that I have made to always be true to my*self* and my values, the energy and time I invested in reflecting on alignment and balance is vast. As a result, I strongly believe that the AWiB experience has greatly contributed to my *self*-development and transformation on the path towards becoming an authentic leader where the process is still underway.

~

CHAPTER EIGHT

Every act, thought, and choice adds to the permanent mosaic: Our decisions ripple through the universe of consciousness to affect the lives of all. Every act or decision made that supports life, supports all life, including our own. ~ David R. Hawkins

8. Wrap-Up: Authentic Leadership and *Self*-Transformation

8.1 Conclusion

This work was inspired by the personal journey I took in adapting and re-settling into the environment and cultural context I had left some years ago. While the initial research topic of choice that brought me back to Ethiopia evolved into a different focus, I believe that the experiences and encounters that have occurred in between my arrival to Ethiopia and the completion of this work, have greatly contributed to the analysis contained in this document. The analysis has been informed by my own personal struggles of living and leading authentically, challenging norms when they become suffocating, and deconstructing through a feminist lens.

With these engines driving the discussion, the purpose that was set at the beginning of this work was to explore authentic leadership and how to cultivate it through *self*-transformation among urban Ethiopian women. In doing so I attempted to draw parallels between the limited literature available on authentic leadership with the near to non-existent research on Ethiopian women's leadership capacities. Given that the very little research focused on Ethiopian women's leadership is heavily weighted at looking at enhancing positional leadership capacities, this work will be a contribution to the field, linking *self*-transformation with authentic leadership development, which I believe both are prerequisites for effectively initiating and managing social change, at whatever level individuals are engaged in.

The leading questions guiding this thesis are captured again below:

1. What are the components of authentic leadership and what type of *self*-transformation is required to be an authentic leader?
2. What is the dominant cultural narrative in Ethiopia which hampers authentic female leadership?
3. How can organized platforms enable *self*-transformation and authentic leadership among urban Ethiopian women?

In answering the first question, I conducted a comprehensive overview of the literature on authentic leadership, focusing more on the leading proponents within the field. I discovered that the literature is still very thin owing to the novelty of authentic leadership as a sub-field in leadership studies. Additionally, as my premise in this work is grounded on the belief that *self*-transformation and authenticity are key to peace practitioners, I also took the route of articulating the transrational approach in peace studies. The transrational rooting in humanistic psychology has also been a basis for linking *self*-transformation and authentic leadership to a peace out of harmony understanding. Furthermore, in responding to what type of *self*-transformation is required to enable authentic female leadership, I studied the intertwining between a *self*-actualization approach to transformation by looking at the triggers and obstacles towards enabling a transformative *self*. I also identified and examined four key components involved in *self*-transformation as well as a deeper analysis of which trigger factors are involved in the transformation of *self*.

Responding to the second question involved examining the literature developed on how culture impacts Ethiopian women's advancement in the various fields they are engaged in. I employed the method of examining through literature research where and how women exercise leadership in the various facets of their lives. The literature on women and culture in Ethiopia also points towards norms that stifle personal and professional growth for many. The findings of the literature review therefore indicate that the dominant cultural narrative which hampers authentic female is attributable to cultural, traditional and religious belief systems which underline how women and girls are socialized in the social fabric of Ethiopia. Additionally, lack of confidence and lack of assertiveness are recorded to be one of the leading obstacles towards exercising authentic leadership among urban women in Ethiopia. Additionally, the feedback received from three women to get a sense of other women's perspective on culture, women and leadership in Ethiopia have also been taken into consideration in responding to the second research question.

The third research question pointed to how organized platforms enable *self*-transformation and authentic leadership among urban Ethiopian women. The analysis in response to this research question is based on an almost two year journey of collecting facts and observable insights into how the case study organization featured in this work, Association of Women in Business (AWiB) enables such transformation to occur. By looking at the leadership and *self*-transformation model that AWiB is continually evolving and emulating, a better understanding of what transformative spaces look like has been achieved. Additionally, in examining AWiB's monthly programmatic activities under the lens of how effective and useful it has been towards enabling *self*-transformation among members and participants, feedback was received from women of different backgrounds who frequent AWiB to assess how they perceived the programs affected their personal development. For the most part, the responses harvested affirm that such transformative spaces are rare in form and inspire transformation.

In the introductory section of this work which aimed to set the background for the analysis behind the research questions posed, it was articulated that the limitations of this study were linked to the identification of a small sub-set of women in Ethiopia who can hardly be said to represent a female population of roughly around 40million. Reintroducing those limitations here again, there is potential for further research in this area. While the purpose of this work was to shed light on this realm of leadership development for peace and personal and social change, its aim is also to inspire other researchers to further examine the various issues that have been brought up in this work as it relates to *self*, leadership and the effect transformative spaces have for such enhancement. There is still so much that is unknown on how women in Ethiopia exercise leadership; how leadership it*self* is understood and performed by both men and women; and how various programmes with the goal of enabling leadership actually impact people at the level of *self*-transformation.

It has been my aim throughout this work to shed the light of consciousness on the importance of enabling female leadership in Ethiopia, specifically through a *self*-transformative approach. I hope that my readers have been able to grasp the red thread weaved throughout this work and understand the source of my passion and energy that I have invested with others, in making a transformative space such as AWiB work its magic of limitless possibilities and unleashing of potential as it has for me.

~

In finalizing this work, I leave my readers with a poem I wrote in 2009 when the light of *self*-transformation had shone its light on me:

In Fields of Abundance

Have I not refused to move forward
And held my*self* in the burning ache of fears
Have I not looked back and seen a reflection
Of a weakened me in a pool of salty tears

Have not the lessons then shed a beam
And made a vineyard of my qualms
Risen have I not from the mental ashes
To a harp have I not sung my personal psalms

Through many journeys has a friend turned into foe
And have I looked at me to see how this became so
When karma beckoned me to build bridges
Have I not in a cycle of samsara rid my heart of ridges

Have I not yet filtered impurities from my soul
And given prominence to the beauty of moments and memories
To weave into my tapestry of being
A continual pattern of inspiriting stories

Have I chosen yet to not be any more
Of empty New Year resolutions
Have I willed rather a life of no restrictions
But vowed instead to live it with the most sincerest of intentions

- Billene Seyoum Woldeyes (December 2009)

~

BIBLIOGRAPHY

Ashenafi, M. (2009). *Participation of Women in Political and Public Decision Making in Ethiopia.* Addis Ababa: Forum for Social Studies.

Avolio, B., & Gardner, W. (2005). Authentic Leadership Development: Getting to the root of positive forms of leadership. *The Leadership Quarterly 16*, 325.

Avolio, B., & Gardner, W. (2005). Authentic Leadership Development: Getting to the root of positive forms of leadership. *The Leadership Quarterly 16*, 318.

Baan, C., Long, P., & Pearlman, D. (n.d.). *The Lotus - A Practice Guide for Authentic Leadership Toward Sustainability.* Retrieved from www.womensplace.osu.edu/assets/files/TheLotus_v1.1_lowres.pdf

Balogh, L. (n.d.). Retrieved from http://doktori.bibl.u-szeged.hu/1518/3/theses.pdf.

Bekele, B. (2012, October 4). Introduction to Appreciative Inquiry.

Berger, J. G. (n.d.). *Key concepts of understanding the work of Robert Kegan.* Retrieved from Shifting Thinking: http://www.shiftingthinking.org/?page_id=449

Biseswar, I. (2008). Problems of Feminist Leadership among Educated Women in Ethiopia: Taking Stock in the Third Millennium. *Journal of Developing Societies.*

Biseswar, I. (2011). The Role of Educated/Intellectual Women in Ethiopia in the Process of Change and Transformation towards Gender Equality 1974-2005. 204.

Bizuneh, B. (2001). Women in Ethiopian History: A Bibliographic Review. *Northeast African Studies 8.3*, 7-32. Retrieved from http://muse.jhu.edu/login?auth=0&type=summary&url=/journals/northeast_african_studies/v008/8.3bizuneh.pdf

Brown, J., Evans, R., Buckely, M., Michael, G., & Novicevic, M. (2006). Authentic Leadership: A Historical Perspective. *Journal of Leadership and Organizational Studies Vol. 13 No. 1*, 66.

Cairn, R. (n.d.). *Adult Consciousness Development.* Retrieved from Rob Cairns Consulting: http://www.robcairnsconsulting.com/articles/adult_consciousness.htm

Condon, R. J. (2011). The Relationship between *Self* Awareness and Leadership: Extending Measurement and Conceptualisation. University of Canterbury.

Dietrich, W. (n.d.). *A Call for Trans-Rational Peaces.* Retrieved from http://www.uibk.ac.at/peacestudies/downloads/peacelibrary/transrational.pdf.

Ditz, N. A. (n.d.). *Self-Actualization, Empowerment & Intimacy.* Retrieved from Holistic Depth Therapy: http://www.holisticdepththerapy.com/areas2.php

Dulany, P. (2012). *Approaching the Heart of the Matter: Personal Transformation the Emergence of New Leadership.* New York: Synergos Institute.

English-Word Information. (2012, December 9). Retrieved from Word Info: http://wordinfo.info/unit/3771/ip:16

Genene, M. (2003). Gender and Leadership Issues for Discussion. *Bridge Building between Ethiopia and Austria* (p. 9). Vienna: Äthiopisch-Österreichische Frauensolidarität.

Gentry, W., Weber, T., & Sadri, G. (n.d.). *Empathy in the Workplace: A Tool for Effective Leadership.* Retrieved from Centre for Creative Leadership: http://www.ccl.org/leadership/pdf/research/EmpathyInTheWorkplace.pdf.

Goleman, D. (2004). What Makes a Leader? *Harvard Business Review*, 3.

Heidegger, M. (2012, December 25). *Our Existential Predicament: Loneliness, Depression, Anxiety, & Death.* . Retrieved from http://www.tc.umn.edu/~parkx032/XP226.html

Hunt, K. (n.d.). *Creativity, Self-Actualization and You.* Retrieved from Kendal Hunt: http://www.kendallhunt.com/samples/3930.pdf.

Hussein, J. W. (n.d.). *A Discursive Representation of Women in Sample Proverbs from Ethiopia, Sudan and Kenya.* Retrieved from http://muse.jhu.edu/journals/ral/summary/v040/40.3.hussein.html.

Jacobsen, B. (2007). Authenticity and Our Basic Existential Dilemmas. . *Existential Analysis: Journal of the Sciences for Existential Analysis 18:2*.

Kegan, R. (1982). *The Evolving Self - Problem and Process in Human Development.* London: Harvard University Press.

Kegan, R. (n.d.). *The Constitutions of the Self*. Retrieved from http://faculty.plts.edu/gpence/2490/html/kegan.htm

Klenke, K. (2007). Authentic Leadership: A *Self*, Leader, and Spiritual Identity Perspective. *International Journal of Leadership Studies, Vol 3, Iss. 1*, 72.

Koppensteiner, N. (2010, July 5). Transrational Interpretations of Peace - Presentation during Modular Period II. Innsbruck, Tirol, Austria: University of Innsbruck.

Ladkin, D., & Taylor, S. (2010). Enacting the 'True *Self*': Towards a Theory of Embodied Authentic Leadership. *The Leadership Quarterly, Volume 21, Issue 1*, 5.

Mazutis, D., & Slawinksi, N. (n.d.). *The Art of Conversation: How Authentic Leaders Influence Organizational Learning.* Retrieved from http://www2.warwick.ac.uk/fac/soc/wbs/conf/olkc/archive/olkc2/papers/mazutis_and_slawinski.pdf.

Mezirow, J. (n.d.). *Transformative Learning: Theory to Practice.* Retrieved from http://www.dlc.riversideinnovationcentre.co.uk/wp-content/uploads/2012/10/Transformative-Learning-Mezirow-1997.pdf.

Quast, L. (n.d.). *Is There Really a Glass Ceiling for Women?* Retrieved from Forbes: http://www.forbes.com/sites/lisaquast/2011/11/14/is-there-really-a-glass-ceiling-for-women/.

Sayer, S. (2012, December 20). *The Concept of Authenticity.* Retrieved from http://www.kent.ac.uk/secl/philosophy/articles/sayers/authenticity.pdf.

Schmid, P. F. (2012, December 15). *Authenticity: The Person as His or Her Own Author. Diological and Ethical Perspectives on Therapy as An Encounter Relationship. And Beyond.* Retrieved from http://web.utanet.at/schmidpp/paper-authent.pdf

Shamir, B., & Eilam, G. (2005). What's your story? A life stories approach to authentic leadership development. . *Leadership Quarterly 16 (3)*.

Sharma, R. (n.d.). *Holden Leadership Centre.* Retrieved from 10 Things Authentic Leaders Do: http://leadership.uoregon.edu/resources/exercises_tips/leadership_reflections/10_things_authentic_leaders_do.

Sparrow, R. T. (2005). Authentic Leadership and the narrative *self*. *The Leadership Quarterly 16*, 429.

Tolle, E. (2005). *A New Earth - Awakening to Your Life's Purpose.* Plume.

Turk, A. C. (n.d.). *Genuine Contact Facilitation.* Retrieved from http://www.gc-facilitation.de/

Waber, N. (n.d.). *Appreciative Inquiry - Getting to Solutions by Looking at What's Going Right.* Retrieved from AWiB: http://awib.org.et/index.php/event-recap/222-appreciative-inquiry-getting-to-solutions-by-looking-at-whats-going-right.

Wagner, T. (n.d.). *Five Hallmarks of Authentic Leaders.* Retrieved from http://southcentral.construction.com/opinions/LeadershipDev/archive/2009/09.asp.

Weberman, D. (2011). Sartre on the Authenticity required if my choices are to be truly mine. *FILOZOFIA 66*, 879. Retrieved from http://www.klemens.sav.sk/fiusav/doc/filozofia/2011/9/879-889.pdf

Woldeyes, B. S. (n.d.). About AWiB. *Script developed in 2012 for AWiB.* . Association of Women in Business (AWiB).

Yukl, G. (2010). *Leadership in Organizations, 7th Edition*. New Jersey: Pearson.

Zelelew, M. (December, 20 2013). *Women in Leadership and Decision-making - The Ethiopian Perspective.* . Retrieved from CRDA Ethiopia: http://www.crdaethiopia.org/genderforum/Documents/Proceedings%20of%20A%20Workshop%20on%20Women%20in%20Leadership%20and%20Decision%20Making.pdf.

Zielinska, M. (n.d.). *Developing Authentic Leadership*. Retrieved from Kenexa: http://www.kenexa.com/Portals/0/Downloads/Developing%20Authentic%20Leaders.pdf

APPENDIX

**Sample blog entries on AWiB web site geared towards inspiring self-transformation.*

BLOG ENTRY SAMPLE I: THE AUTHENTICITY OF PERSONAL POWER BY BILLENE SEYOUM

I wholeheartedly believe in the wisdom of children because they live their truth every day and live it unpretentiously. I also believe that we give these little human beings less credit than they deserve for their wisdom and the audacity with which they exist. My now four-year old niece is proof of that. And anyone that knows me well knows how often I talk about her in amazement. As a three-year old she would speak with the assertiveness and honesty that I often find lacking in the adult world. She is a little girl who knows what she wants when she wants it, and nothing can compromise her conviction. She is truly a child that honours her feelings and one that cannot be coerced into action even through promises that often distract little children.

The reason I share this story is in reflection of what it means to have personal power. On the evening of Maski's session on "*The Mysticism of Personal Power*" an audience member shared that personal power meant *"to be with myself and be able to travel the path I choose to travel"*. This profound statement which strongly resonated with me made me question how many of us truly travel the path we choose and do that consistently. I equate traveling the path of our choice with claiming authenticity or operating in alignment with our core essence, rather than in seeking external validation.

How many times have you done something you did not want to do? Or held your*self* back from expressing your truth which lies simmering wildly within you underneath a demeanour of fabricated *self*-content? How many times have you restrained your*self* wondering how your peers and "others" would perceive you? Or adopted 'herd mentality' so as to not stand out and be the black sheep?

For me these are all expressions of denying ourselves authenticity in our actions and interactions. They rob us of our personal power because falling in line with actions and interactions which are not in alignment with our essence and feelings, takes away some form of energy from us. And that which depletes and does not replenish our energy is that which tires us and curbs the enthusiasm we have for future action and engagement. So why continue?

How about reclaiming our personal power by staying true to ourselves? How about closely looking at the three-year olds in our lives or around us and learning a thing or two about living authentically? How about allowing our inner-child to grow with us rather than against us?

So what do you think about the authenticity of personal power?

BLOG ENTRY SAMPLE II: GROWING IN SKILLS, GROWING IN BEING BY NADIA WABER

I smile when I reflect on what drew me to join a network such as AWiB! I feel stimulated, alive and hopeful when I attend the events and meetings. And I wonder, what's behind that buzz I sense inside?

I would say that it's the experience of the wonderful impulse of GROWTH. Indeed, being a member (and board member) of the Association of Women in Business (AWiB) has enabled me to stretch and:

- Cultivate my newly acquired business skills,
- Rediscover the power of networking, to connect with and seek support from some very vibrant members of our society,
- Contribute in the shaping and growing of this novel organization,
- Grow my skills in enrolling others into the Association's vision, by promoting its benefits and being present to each member's need and hopes when joining,
- Resurface my past skills in Public Relations and Communications, and
- Unveil my passion for communicating new ideas through writing, the AWiB website, and other social media.

What an extraordinary opportunity to expand my skills-set! I would say that growing in skills is not just a pleasure, but a necessity these days, given national and global trends which call us to be more agile, creative and pro-active professionals and human beings.

The growth I have described can be called this HORIZONTAL GROWTH in adult development, which refers to expansion in capacities through increases in knowledge, skills, and behaviours associated with a *current mind-set*. There also exists a way we can grow VERTICALLY, and that is through a change/ growth in attitude and mind-set. Thanks to my engagement with this network, I:

- Feel I have new, broader perspectives on the potentials of the business sector in Ethiopia,
- Have developed a new intention to create spaces for young female entrepreneurs to thrive and grow,

- Appreciate the complexity of what it means to manage and lead a business in Ethiopia and in the world.

I trust that such growth in me will enable me to act as a more effective and relevant leader in our society. And I'm curious: through your engagement with AWiB, or similar networks locally or abroad, what new skills have you developed? And how have you grown in attitude, mind-set and intention?

BLOG ENTRY SAMPLE III - HOW DO YOU DETERMINE YOUR *SELF*-WORTH: EXPRESSIONS OF *SELF*-ESTEEM BY SEBLE HAILU

As a counsellor, I hear many loud and soft voices of people as they describe and treat themselves and allow others to treat them. Hence, I would like to start addressing underlying issues that affects our relationships and performances.

Self-esteem is commonly defined as the person's overall evaluation of his or her own worth. This encompasses the belief system which made him/her feel competent or incompetent; the emotional reaction pride or shame; and the behaviour which is reflected on how one conducts him*self*/her*self*.

Some people try to determine their worth by their work, achievements or successes. This has major flaw because it makes *self*-esteem contingent to one's success. If importance is given to individuals by the ratio of one success over failures, this implies inherent instability of *self*-worth because failure can occur at any moment. Some would show their wealth and expect people to bow down for them and yet deep inside, they feel empty for wealth does not fill in one's worth. Same thing applies to gaining more education and power to determine *self*-worth.

Psychologist Alice Mary Hilton stated that how we view ourselves should not be dependent on external factors but on who we are. "A person's worth is contingent upon who he is, not upon what he does, or how much he has. The worth of a person, or a thing, or an idea, is in being, not in doing, not in having." Many psychologists agree *self*-esteem is not an inborn factor rather it develops in earlier years of development process. How parents raise their kids and the impressions they give to their children is imprinted in their kids' lives and that will later be translated in how the kids value themselves as inferior or superior. Alfred Adler, European psychiatrist, wrote that everyone has feelings of inferiority. Sometimes these feelings stimulate us to healthy actions and achievements, but inferiority feelings can also be overwhelming that they cause us to withdraw from others and develop what Adler called an "Inferiority Complex."

People who feel inadequate and inferior tend to compare themselves unfavourably to others. Such comparisons can lead to a lot of human misery and feelings of inadequacy. Some suggest that we can overcome these feelings by developing a positive and healthy *self*-esteem. Family Therapist, Virginia Satir writes, "The crucial factor in what happens both inside people and between people is the picture of individual worth that each person carries around with him."

Real feelings of inferiority comes when parents repeatedly: criticize, shame, reject, scold, set unrealistic standards and goals; express the expectations that the child probably will fail; punish repeatedly and harshly; imply that children are a nuisance, stupid or incompetent or when they overprotect or dominate children so they fail later when forced to be on their own. Insults and belittling comments told in the growing up process can affect how we view ourselves, the way we appear to others, or the artificial lifestyles we build, how we hide from others behind the façade and the way we conduct our lives.

In addition to the parent child relationship, causes of inferiority and low *self*-esteem include: past experiences of failures, wrong doing and guilt, unrealistic expectations, faulty thinking, and unmet *self* and community standards.

Low *self*-esteem can have a wide influence. Everybody feels inferior at times, but when these feelings are intense and long-lasting, virtually all human actions, feelings, attitudes, thoughts and values are affected. Effects of inferiority and low *self*-esteem may result in some feeling isolated and unlovable; too week to overcome their deficiencies and lack the drive/motivation to defend themselves; have difficulty getting along with others; be submissive, dependent and so sensitive that their feelings are hurt easily. Some have lower curiosity or creativity others are less inclined to disclose themselves to others. Lowered *self*-esteem and inferiority also may contribute to a lack of inner peace and security; low *self*-confidence; social withdrawal; jealousy and criticisms of others, interpersonal conflict, *self*-criticism, *self*-hatred and *self*-rejection and depression.

The other extreme is to have a strong drive to gain power, superiority or control over others, a tendency to be complaining, argumentative, intolerant, hypersensitive, and unforgiving; inability to accept complements or expressions of love and an inclination to be a poor listener. Having arrogant, haughty estimation of one*self* in relation to others arise from trying to fill in one's emptiness. Superiority complex may also refer to the unrealistic and exaggerated belief that one is better than others. In some people, this develops as a way to compensate for unconscious feelings of low *self*-esteem or inadequacy. For example, bullies who push other children around act like they are stronger and smarter than others their age. Sometimes, the reality is that they simply have low *self*-esteem and bully others in order to compensate for their perceived lack of *self*-worth. Some bosses may put on a tough facade and try to make others think well of them, but inside they feel inadequate and do not respect themselves. Therefore, those exhibiting the superiority complex may project their feelings of inferiority onto others whom they perceive as lesser ones, possibly for the same reasons for which they themselves may have been ostracized. Husbands who use their financial, physical, or educational power to dominate their wives usually suffer from low *self*-esteem and they use force to compensate for their low *self*-esteem. Some ladies over decorate themselves and be seen as all together to fill in the low *self*-esteem. Hence, low *self*-esteem has different manifestations for different people.

Feelings of inferiority build up over many years. Dealing with this does not bring about change immediately, but over a period of time. As a counsellor, I can easily pick that up in the underlying messages people convey and help in assuring clients as they seek to develop understanding of the roots of those behaviours and encourage that people who have low *self*-esteem do not need to be prisoners of their past, rather they can change as they understand the root causes and deal with them.

Proper *self*-love and respect is essential in order to extend that to others. This does not equate with the attitude of superiority, stubborn *self*-will or *self*-centred pride; nor is it an ecstatic *self*-adoration. It is the way to see and accept ourselves the way we are. It is not *self*ishness.

Many people suffer from inferiority complex just because they would never measure up to the parents' standards or that of the societies. We spare ourselves from dealing with many people who live in a *self*-made façade world, constantly need to prove themselves or try to feel their emptiness by lofty gains if we give value for people just because of who they are - unconditional acceptance of *self* and others. Our *self*-worth does not depend on our achievements or lack of it. If we start valuing ourselves because we are created worthy, that is the beginning point to respect others worth, rights and differences.

I want to encourage especially women to see their worth in their womanhood, and then stretch to build their *self*-esteem by living for what they believe in. Do not be entangled in finding your worth in relationships, educational achievements, material wealth, and power over others. Your worth is in who you are as a person. You are worthy to live, to be who you are, to achieve what you want to, to stretch your*self* to discover your potential and to contribute to the wellbeing of others. However, those things would not determine your worth; for you are more valuable than your achievement or lack of it.

My Conclusion is that the origin of *self*-esteem is home. This gives great responsibility to parents and guardians in taking precaution not to end up giving unintended messages to their kids which is persistent through adulthood. Do we value children so that they value themselves, not because of what they might do but because of who they are?

My challenge for each individual is to examine the underlying reasons for how you regard your*self*. This affects every aspect of your behaviour, your ability to learn, your capacity to grow and change; the way you relate with others and the way you present and conduct your*self*.

BLOG ENTRY SAMPLE IV – IN DOING SO BY NAHU S. GIRMA

On a Sunday afternoon, I am reflecting on a successful event I helped organize for AWiB. Association of Women in Business (AWiB) is a young and dynamic association that strives to develop women leaders in Ethiopia. The event was to celebrate great Ethiopians for their immense contribution to their community -- "Women of Excellence". As a founder and president of AWiB, most responsibilities as a leader, naturally fell on my plate. But I had great help from the 13 dynamic and committed board members that AWiB is blessed with. It was fun and was a very successful event.

This was a dream I had for a long time… when I start a networking group that allows women of purpose to come together and to create… my dream was also to celebrate those who have done this creation in their lives without the benefit of a platform such as AWiB. I succeeded in both.

Many who know me and my tenacity for every meaningful endeavour ask me what my drive is. And I say it is more like a commitment. So, dear readers, I want to tell you a bit about commitment and through my brief analysis you get to know me a bit.

The most important factor for individual success is commitment. Commitment sparks action....then results will follow. Commitment is a personal thing that each of us must face every day. Being committed and staying committed is a mind-set that each of us must address in our lives if we want to become a success. Commitment also requires a strong belief in what we do. The pillar of our being is founded strongly in a strong belief of what we do must be done. I believe that's the tenet for my success.

Without commitment nothing happens. I see many in our community start something and don't follow it with action. Lack of commitment is the malaise that has plagued our life and prevents us from what we want to be; where we want to go and who we want to take with us. Rather we have become spectators with many nay sayers and surprised when someone gets it. "Women of Excellence", the event I am talking about involved many and wasn't easy or simple. It involved emotional as well as physical investment. But I knew it would be successful because I was committed to its success. I was not surprised but the reaction of many made me realize no one did believe it would fly.

A certain Steve Pavlina concludes commitment for me and I would like to use this excerpt from him:

> *Put your head underwater and keep it there for a while. You'll soon realize that you're 100% committed to breathing. Notice that you don't make excuses not to breathe. Notice that you don't worry about motivating yourself to breathe. Notice that you don't need to justify your desire to breathe. You just breathe.*

Commitment is action. No excuses. No debate. No lengthy analysis. No whining about how hard it is. No worrying about what others might think. No cowardly delays. Just go. What if something gets in the way of your commitment? What would you do if someone tried to prevent you from breathing?

Fortunately, paying the price that commitment commands has payoffs worth the cost - a reputation for integrity and, even more important, the commitment of others in return. Commitment is a two-way street. You only get it if you are willing to give it. So, dear readers, if you want to succeed, Commit!

ABOUT

Billene Seyoum Woldeyes is a writer and poet based in Addis Ababa, Ethiopia. She is currently a Program Manager at the Synergos Institute working on building leadership capacity for systems-shifting collaborations in the agricultural sector. She holds two MA's - one in Gender & Peacebuilding from the University of Peace, Costa Rica and another in Peace Studies & Conflict Transformation from the University of Innsbruck, Austria. Billene is the immediate past president (2013) of the Association of Women in Business (AWiB) – a membership association focused on developing female leadership through personal and professional development. She is also a feminist blogger at African Feminism – www.africanfeminism.com.

Masters of Peace

edited by Prof. Dr. Wolfgang Dietrich (UNESCO Chair for Peace Studies)

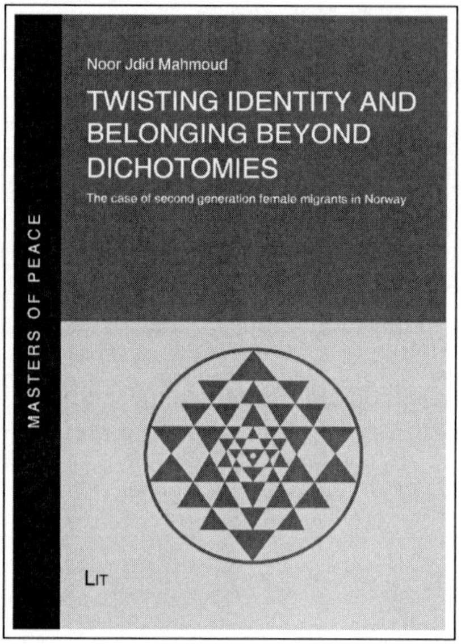

Noor Jdid Mahmoud
Twisting Identity and Belonging beyond Dichotomies
The case of second generation female migrants in Norway

This book brings together personal stories and theoretical concepts in the exploration of how second generation female migrants (SGFMs) in Norway negotiate their identities and give new form and content to their own notions of peace and belonging beyond a double life. By applying postmodern and feminist scholarship, the author challenges static ideas of cultural identity in discourses about the national and the family contexts. Mahmoud takes the reader on a journey through the transformations of conflicts on sexuality, identity and belonging by the SGFMs themselves. This is an important book for feminist and migration researchers and those concerned with minority issues.

Bd. 8, 2013, 168 S., 19,90 €, br., ISBN 978-3-643-90356-3

Kathleen McGoey
Harmonizing Heavens and Earth
A Daoist Shamanic Approach to Peacework

This book explores how shamanic Daoist practices help cultivate the skills of an elicitive peaceworker. The author uses embodied writing to describe her direct experiences with qigong and other meditation forms, and explain the creation of inner peace that ultimately extends far beyond the individual. A transrational understanding of peace weaves together transpersonal interpretations of intuition with ancient Daoist wisdom. By relating the outcomes of such approaches to real world conflict transformation, McGoey proposes a practical personal consciousness that strives for harmony with others and our environments.

Bd. 9, 2013, 208 S., 24,90 €, br., ISBN 978-3-643-90455-3

LIT Verlag Berlin – Münster – Wien – Zürich – London
Auslieferung Deutschland / Österreich / Schweiz: siehe Impressumsseite